Animals and Their Secrets

Ducks!

...And Their Secrets: A Book For Curious Kids and Families

Joanna Slodownik

What's inside

Part 1. Fun Facts about Ducks 3
Ducks, Swans and Geese Are One Family 4
Physical Characteristics of Ducks 8
A Duck, a Swan, or a Goose: Who is Who? 10
Why Do Swans Have Such a Long Neck? 13
Ducks are Descendants of Dinosaurs! 14
Why Do Ducks Lay Eggs? 20
Duck Habitat: Where Do Ducks Live? 28
Are Ducks Endangered? 35
Quack! Quack! Say what? 39
Where Do the Wild Ducks Go in Winter? 44
How Are Ducks Similar to People? 46
Part 2. The Hidden Lives of Ducks 52
Not Fun Facts about Duck Farms 53
Eat, Drink, and Poop 56
Biodiversity and Ducks 57
The Herbivore Diet 60
Part 3. Should Ducks Have Rights? 68
Duck Sayings: how many do you know? 74
Quiz Time! 79
Read More Books 83

While every precaution has been taken in the preparation of this book, the publisher assumes no responsibility for errors or omissions, or for damages resulting from the use of the information contained herein.

DUCKS! AND THEIR SECRETS. A BOOK FOR CURIOUS KIDS AND FAMILIES

First edition. January 15, 2023.

This Amazing World Press

Copyright © 2023 Joanna Slodownik; Written by Joanna Slodownik.

Part 1.
Fun Facts about Ducks

Ducks are awesome!

Ducks are caring, sensitive, and very intelligent birds.

That's right! Those who take the time to get to know them better can testify that ducks are fantastic animals.

It is never too early—or too late—to learn more about these birds and discover their deeply hidden secrets.

So, let's begin!

Ducks, swans and geese are one family!

Ducks are not one species of animal. All types of ducks are part of the bird family Anatidae, which also includes swans and geese. What do swans, geese, and ducks have in common? They are all waterfowl. Waterfowl are birds that live on or near water that have **webbed feet and broad, flat beaks, called bills.** These types of birds are known as Anseriformes, which comprise at least 166 species, though some may be extinct.

The Anatidae are adapted for swimming, floating on the water surface, and diving in shallow water. They live on every continent of the world except for Antarctica, where it's too cold. Some species, such as the Mallard, are found around the world, while others have small, restricted ranges.

Most domesticated ducks descend from wild Mallard ducks. Wikipedia lists 83 breeds of domestic ducks, but there are probably hundreds of domestic duck breeds.

Scientific name: Anatidae
Lifespan*: Mallard: 5 - 10 years, Canada goose: 10 - 24 years,
Swan: 20 years (*Most ducks raised for their flesh live only 7 weeks.)
Kingdom: Animalia
Order: Anseriformes
Phylum: Chordata

Physical characteristics of ducks

Ducks love the water! They are semi-aquatic birds. A semi-aquatic animal is an animal that lives partly on land and partly in the water. Ducks spend most of their time on and around water, but they also can spend a lot of time on land. Water allows ducks to keep themselves clean and helps them with eating. If ducks eat and do not have access to water, they could choke. Plus, they can find so many things to eat in the water. Ducks can live in salt water or freshwater environments. They are found in wetlands, marshes, ponds, rivers, lakes and oceans. This is the reason they are called **waterfowl.**

Ducks have **waterproof feathers**. Ducks naturally produce a special waterproof oil, which they rub all over their feathers with their beaks. It's called **preening**. When ducks are preening, they are grooming their feathers and applying the oil. Without it, their feathers would not be waterproof. Once they apply the oil, the feathers closest to their skin stay dry even in the water. This helps ducks stay warm. Another amazing thing that helps ducks do so well in the water is their **webbed feet.** Without the webbed feet, ducks wouldn't be able to move so well in the water.

Ducks can be different colors, shapes, and sizes. Baby ducks are called **ducklings**. Female ducks are called **hens**. Male ducks are called **drakes**. Drakes are often brightly colored, and can be red, green, brown, or black, or other. Hens are usually brown or white. Duck feet change color during the mating season, when they turn a bright red. Then they turn a dull color again to blend into their surroundings. Ducks do not have external ears, as we do. The ears are just openings into the ear canal, and are protected by a covering of feathers.

Ducks' webbed feet are like flippers, helping them swim.

How to tell if a duck is male or female?

Telling the difference between male and female birds takes keen observation and paying close attention to the details. Not all species have easy-to-spot differences between genders, but it is often possible to recognize which birds are male or female by their appearance.

Many bird species are **dimorphic**, meaning that males and females look different. Usually, male birds sport brighter colors to be more attractive to females, while females are usually less colorful, so they can easier blend into the surroundings when they sit on eggs or protect their young. Many duck species have very colorful male plumages but camouflaged females.

These differences are most visible during the breeding season in spring and summer. Even with bold colors, males can quite easily blend into bright flowers and foliage during these months. For some species, males change to a more subdued plumage each fall but will return to their brighter colors in the spring.

Sexual dimorphism is when males and females of the same species have different characteristics, especially those not directly related to reproduction. Dimorphism occurs in most animals and some plants.

Some species, such as mute swan, are not dimorphic, and instead can be distinguished by other characteristics. Generally, male mute swans, or cobs, are taller and larger than females, or pens, and have thicker necks and a 'knob' above their bill. Measuring 50 to 63 inches in length (125 to 160 cm), this large swan is all white in plumage with an orange beak bordered with black. The name 'mute' comes from it being less vocal than other swan species.

Mute swans

Can you spot the female ducks in the photos below?

Mandarin ducks, female and males

Mergus merganser, female and male

Mallard ducks, female and male

A duck, a swan, or a goose: who is who?

Geese, swans and ducks are one family, so how can we tell them apart? Why is a duck a duck and not a swan or a goose? The primary way taxonomists (scientists who study how living things are related to each other) differentiate between ducks, geese, and swans is based on the number of cervical vertebrae, or how many neck bones they have. **Ducks have 16 or fewer bones in their necks, geese have 17 to 23 neck bones, and swans have 24 or more. That's more than a giraffe!** Of course, there is no way we can easily count birds' bones, so how can we tell who is who?

Swans are larger and heavier than ducks. Ducks feathers come in a wide variety of colors and patterns, while swans are solid in color, usually white or black. The Northern Hemisphere species of swan have pure white feathers, but the Southern Hemisphere species are mixed black and white. The Australian black swans are all black except for the white feathers on their wings. Swan chicks' plumage is gray.

Geese are also on average larger than ducks and have longer bodies as well as longer legs, but their necks aren't as long as swans'. Ducks are usually smaller than geese and have shorter bodies and legs.

Why do swans have such a looong neck?

Swans are famous for their beauty, majesty, and grace. But why do they need such a long neck? Swans **use their long neck to find food at the bottom of the lake or river bed that they would not be able reach otherwise**. They eat aquatic plants, small fish, mollusks, and other invertebrates. Swans' flexible necks allow them to move their head freely in all directions, even turning it 180 degrees. Thanks to their necks, they can forage under water, on the water's edge, and on land.

> Swans are benthic foragers. A benthic forager is an animal that finds food on or near the bottom of a body of water. The word *benthic* comes from ancient Greek, meaning "the depths."

Although giraffe's neck can be eight feet long, it only has 7 neck vertebrae, the same number as humans! However, unlike human or swan's neck bones, each of theirs can be up to 10 inches long.

Ducks are living descendants of dinosaurs!

Ducks are the closest living relative to the T-Rex. That's right! Scientists found evidence that has proven the shared common ancestry between birds and the *Tyrannosaurus rex*.

You may have enjoyed the Jurassic Park movie and wished you could see those reptiles for yourself—and you can! There are real dinosaurs just outside your window, only we call them birds!

Birds belong to the theropod group of dinosaurs that included *T. rex*. *Archaeopteryx*, discovered in 1861, is considered a transitional species closest to the origin of birds. It lived during the Late Jurassic era (about 150 million years ago). Other dinosaurs closely related to birds, like *Velociraptor*, can be from the Late Cretaceous (100- 66 million years ago). Not all of the dinosaurian close relatives of birds could fly.

A feathered dinosaur is any species of dinosaur with feathers. It's possible that many, if not all non-avian dinosaur species also had feathers.

Feathers' original function may had been thermal insulation, before their modification in birds into structures that support flight.

Since scientific research began on dinosaurs in the early 1800s, they were believed to be closely related to modern reptiles, such as lizards. The word 'dinosaur,' first used in 1842 by paleontologist Richard Owen, comes from the Greek for **'terrible lizard'**. Later on researchers found evidence that dinosaurs were much more closely related to birds, which descended directly from the theropod group of dinosaurs.

Illustration depicting an individual of Acheroraptor with pennaceous feathers

So what do you think? Is there family likeness?

What do ducks eat?

Ducks love to bob for their food, which consists mostly of small plants, tasty fish, and yummy insects. **Some heavier ducks can dive really deep to catch fish.** They're called diving ducks. **The ducks' bill is extremely sensitive.** It's like ducks have a million finger tips all along it. The bill, helps a duck discover food and filters out stuff that the duck doesn't want to eat like mud. So, the beak finds food, snags the food, and filters it, and then the duck swallows what's inside.

Have you ever seen a duck do this? Ducks often dunk their heads underwater to feast on things in the water, such as plants, insects, and fish. Bext time you see ducks with their heads underwater, just know that they're looking for something yummy to eat.

No one ever called a duck a picky eater! Ducks are omnivorous and will eat grass, water plants, worms, grain, seeds, nuts, fruit, insects, small fish, and pretty much anything else they can get their beaks on. This opportunistic eating helps ensure they always have plenty of food to eat. Waterfowl have only about 400 taste buds, which is not very many, but enough to allow them distinguish between certain flavors. Humans have 9,000 taste buds, while catfish have about 100,000! Now that's a lot of buds!

Many people have seen what look like teeth lining the edges of duck's or goose's beaks and mistaken them for teeth.

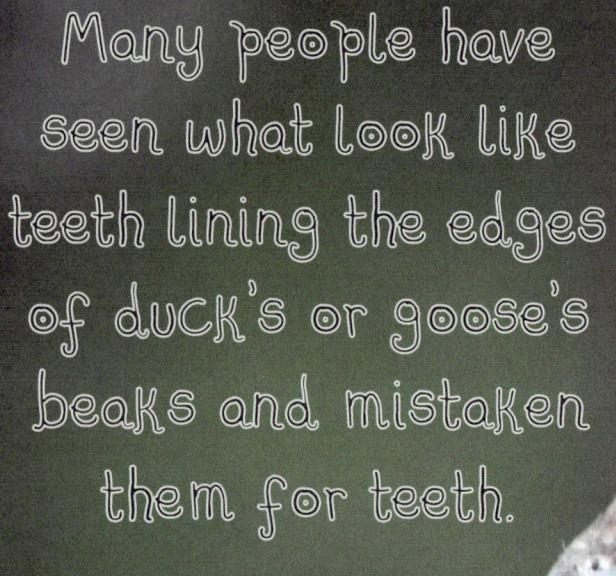

But, like all birds, ducks and geese don't have teeth. Instead, they have hard structures called lamellae around the edges of their bills.

Why do ducks swallow sharp rocks and gravel?

To grind up the seeds and bones of the fish that they swallow whole! That's right! These pieces of rocks and pebbles that birds eat are called gastroliths.

Gastroliths are small pieces of gravel, rocks, or sand that birds eat and store in their gizzard.

Today's birds don't have teeth, but scientists found fossils of birds that had teeth just like the dinosaurs. So what happened? This was likely an evolutionary modification for flight. Without teeth and jaws, birds became lighter.

But modern birds don't just fly; they need to eat, as well. So, how do they break down tough seeds and other foods? Instead of teeth modern birds have beaks and gizzards! Gizzard is a muscular chamber of the stomach that can break up almost anything inside.

The bird's stomach consists of two parts: a small, thin-walled stomach that secretes digestive enzymes and acid and a larger, thick-walled gizzard. Birds that feed on soft foods, such as fruits have a weakly developed gizzard. Birds that eat seeds, mollusks, or other hard objects, have a gizzard whose walls are thick masses of muscle that contract with tremendous force. The lining of the gizzard is very tough and keeps regenerating itself. Once the rocks are not sharp anymore, birds vomit them and look for new ones. Chickens, turkeys, grouse, and quails, as well as ducks, emus and doves commonly swallow stones.

Why do ducks lay eggs?

Ducks lay eggs to reproduce and have offspring; that's how all birds reproduce. The process of making and laying an egg is very taxing, requiring a lot of energy and labor, so wild ducks lay only 10 to 15 eggs per year, in one to two clutches of eggs per year, with 4 to 6 eggs per clutch on average. Their bodies could never withstand the physical depletion of laying the hundreds of eggs that birds living on farms are forced to produce through genetic manipulation.

It is a common misconception that ducks and chickens are always just naturally "giving us" eggs, because modern egg hens and ducks have been intensively bred to lay between 250 to 300 eggs per year.
In the wild, birds lay eggs only during breeding season—usually in the spring—and only enough eggs to ensure the survival of their genes.

Ducks raised on commercial farms typically lay 300-350 eggs per year, even more eggs than commercial chickens. Large chicken eggs weigh 24-26 ounces per dozen while duck eggs weigh 32-34 ounces per dozen.

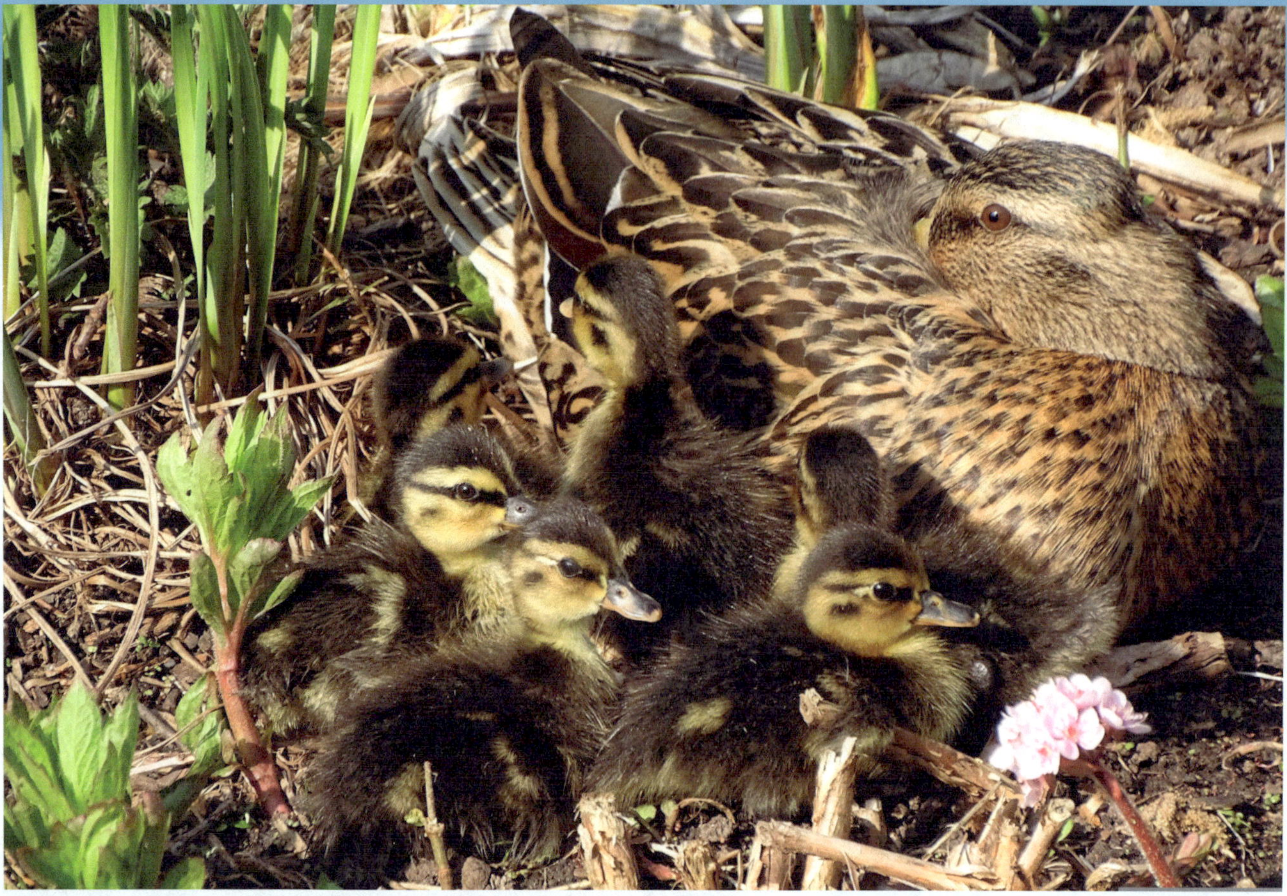

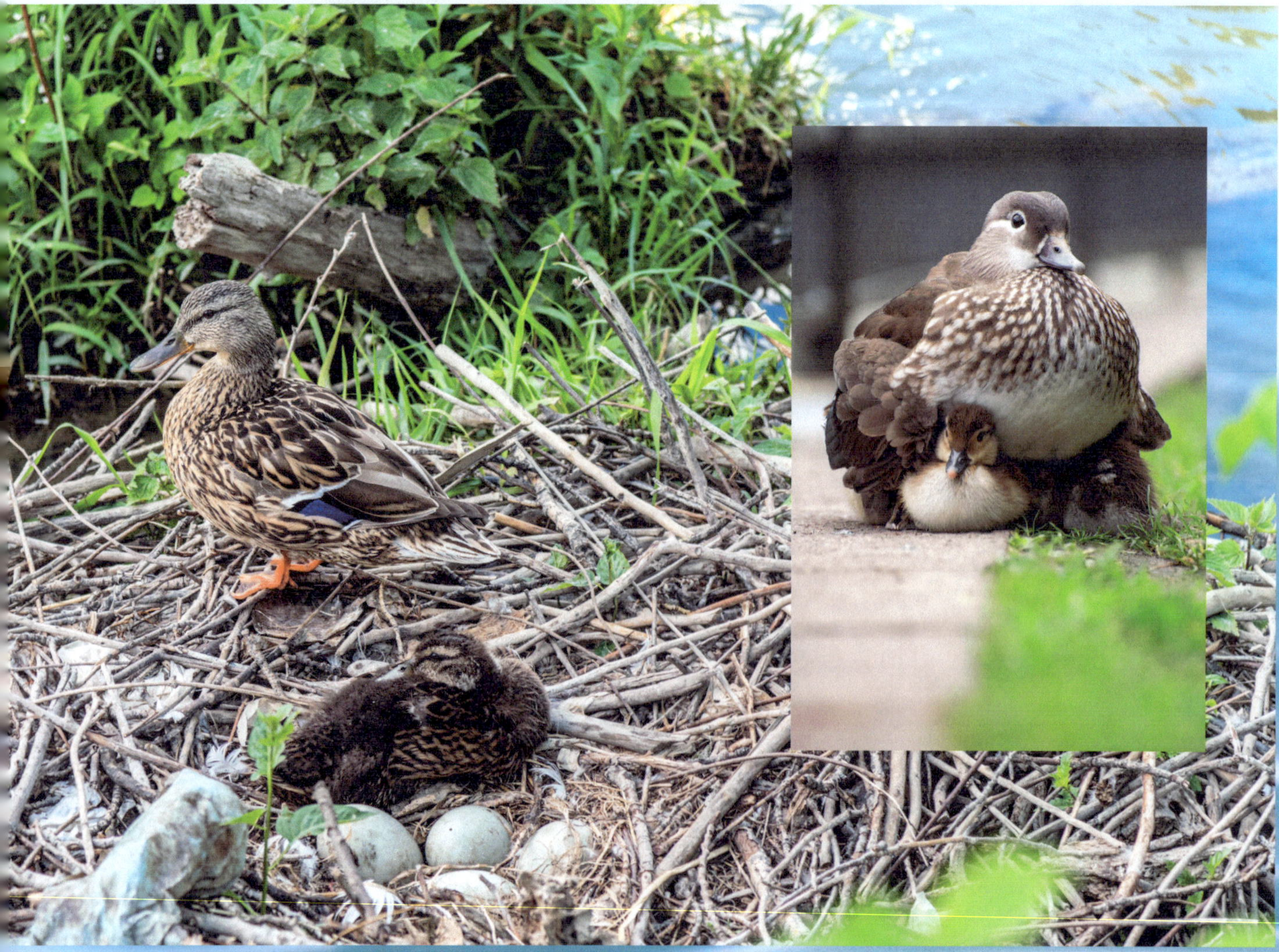

How many eggs do ducks lay?

Once the female duck builds the nest from nearby vegetation, she lays the eggs and stays in the nest to incubate them for about 30 days. Ducks lay 8–13 eggs, and then sit on their eggs to warm them enough for the embryos to grow inside the shell.

What is inside the egg? An embryo!

Each egg provides enough nutrients for the embryo to develop into a healthy duckling. Ducks will sit on their eggs for *up to 23 hours per day* in order to keep them warm.

Incubation is the process in which a bird keeps her eggs warm until the young come out, or the process in which an egg develops until the stage at which the young come out.

Hatching means to produce young by incubation. When a baby bird, insect, or other animal hatches, *it comes out of its egg by breaking the shell*. Ducklings are super cute and tiny when they hatch. Their mother leads them to the water, and right away the ducklings can swim.

Precocial means capable of independent activity from birth.

23

Ducklings rely on their moms for everything—warmth, safety, learning how to eat and drink, and other things they need to survive. The special bond between mother and her ducklings begins before the eggs even hatch.

Life is tough for little ducklings

Many ducklings won't make it to adulthood. A good habitat protects the duck family from bad weather and predators. But with humans building more cities and draining wetlands, good habitats are hard to find. A duckling is also the perfect prey for many predators. Hawks, foxes, snakes, and turtles are all dangerous. These baby birds are almost helpless until they reach maturity and learn to fly.

A few words of caution

Never feed a nesting duck. She does not need food, because she bulked up before laying the eggs. A nesting duck can even not eat for the whole time she is sitting on her eggs. Leaving food around such as bread can attract predators that may eat the eggs and destroy the nest.

Occasionally, a duck may build a nest in a place that the ducklings will not be able to get out of. In these cases, contact wildlife services. If the ducklings have already hatched, provide a shallow bowl of water for them until they can be moved to a safe location by a professional.

Don't feed a nesting duck!

What to do when you find a nest?

In spring nesting season, you may stumble upon a duck nest in the wild. What looks like a bad spot to you may be fine for the duck, and moving the nest may cause more harm than good to the duck and the eggs.

If you find a duck's nest, do not handle it or interfere with it in any way!

A duck may not recognize her nest if it is moved, even just a short distance. Once moved, the nest will be abandoned, so never touch the nest. Any disruptions could cause the mother duck to come off the eggs while they are being incubated, so leave her alone. If she leaves the nest repeatedly or for extended periods of time, the eggs may not hatch.

Mallards are protected under the Migratory Bird Treaty Act of 1918. It is illegal to take, possess, transport, sell, or purchase them or their parts, such as feathers, nests, or eggs, without a permit. Mallard ducks choose their nesting locations carefully. They typically nest on dry ground near water, but look for a spot where they can be safe, sheltered or hidden among the vegetation. If you find a nest that seems to be in a location that's not safe because it's near a parking lot, busy road, or a sidewalk, it's best to tape off the area and put up a sign to alert passers-by to the nest.

Where do wild ducks live?

Every species of duck, goose and swan in North America depends on wetland habitat throughout their life cycle. Ducks' prime habitat is areas of water like **ponds, lakes, marshes, rivers, streams, and even oceans**. They sometimes sleep in a nest made in tall grass near a body of water. Other times they sleep while actually floating on the water!

A marsh is **a type of wetland with soil that is rich in minerals**. Marshes are very similar to swamps. The difference between them is the types of plant life they support. Marshes have mostly grasses, rushes, or reeds, while swamps have mostly trees. The water in freshwater marshes is usually **one to six feet deep** and is rich in minerals. Water flows into marshes from rain or from a water source, like creeks, streams, or rivers. Low-growing plants like grasses and sedges are common in freshwater marshes.

What are wetlands and why are they important?

Wetlands are areas where water covers the soil, or is present either at or near the surface of the soil periodically or all year. Wetlands include marshes, swamps, peat bogs, and similar areas. Although they cover only about 6% of the Earth's surface, they provide habitat to over 40% of the world's species.

Wetlands are among the most biologically diverse ecosystems in the world. The plants, water and soils of wetlands provide homes for a diverse range of species, such as mammals, birds, plants, fish, crustaceans and mollusks. Bacteria, algae and decaying plants create a "wetland soup," a rich breeding ground for all life, leading to an incredible diversity and abundance of larger creatures that are higher up the food chain. Ducks are among the 140 species of birds that depend on wetlands in North America.

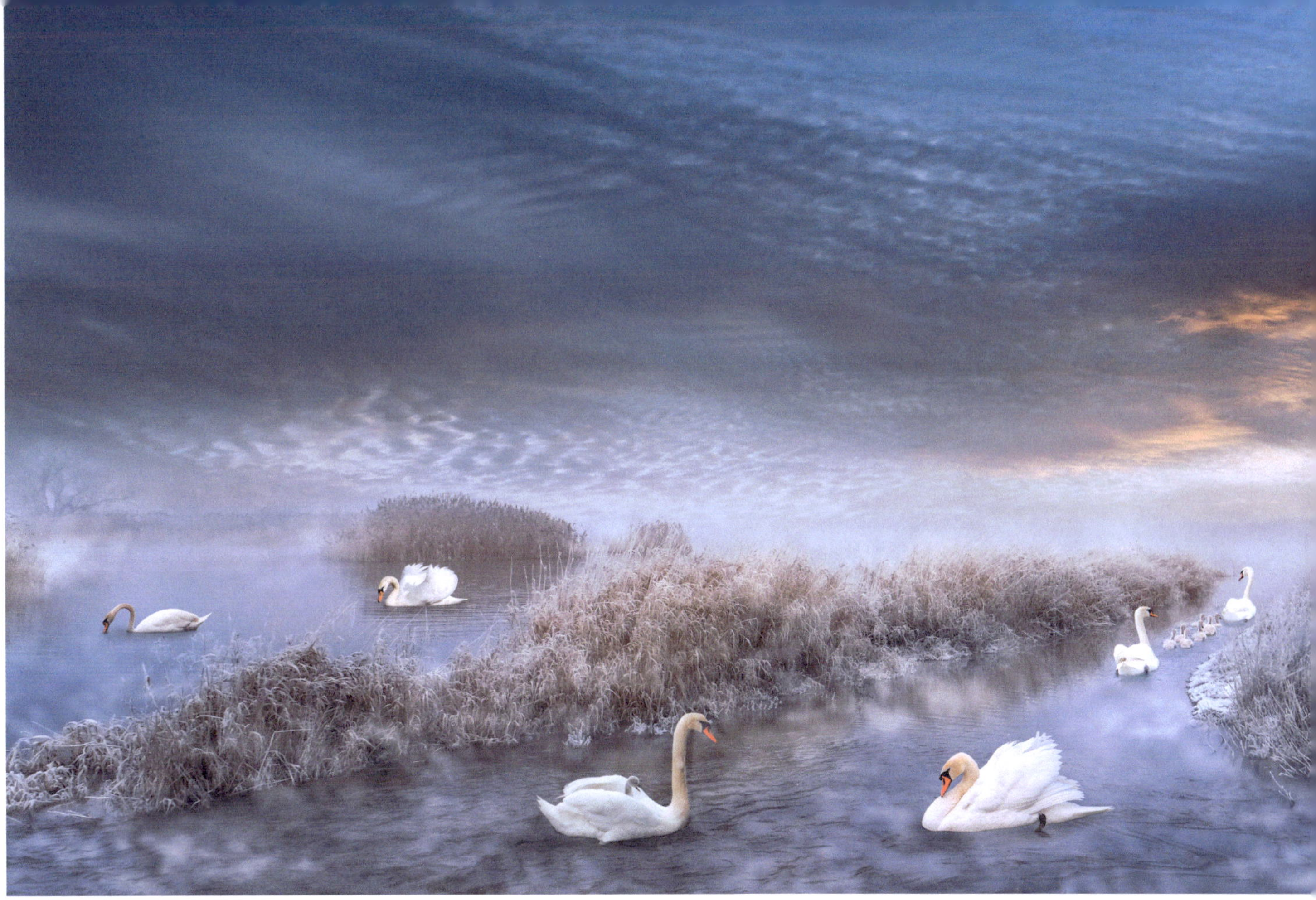

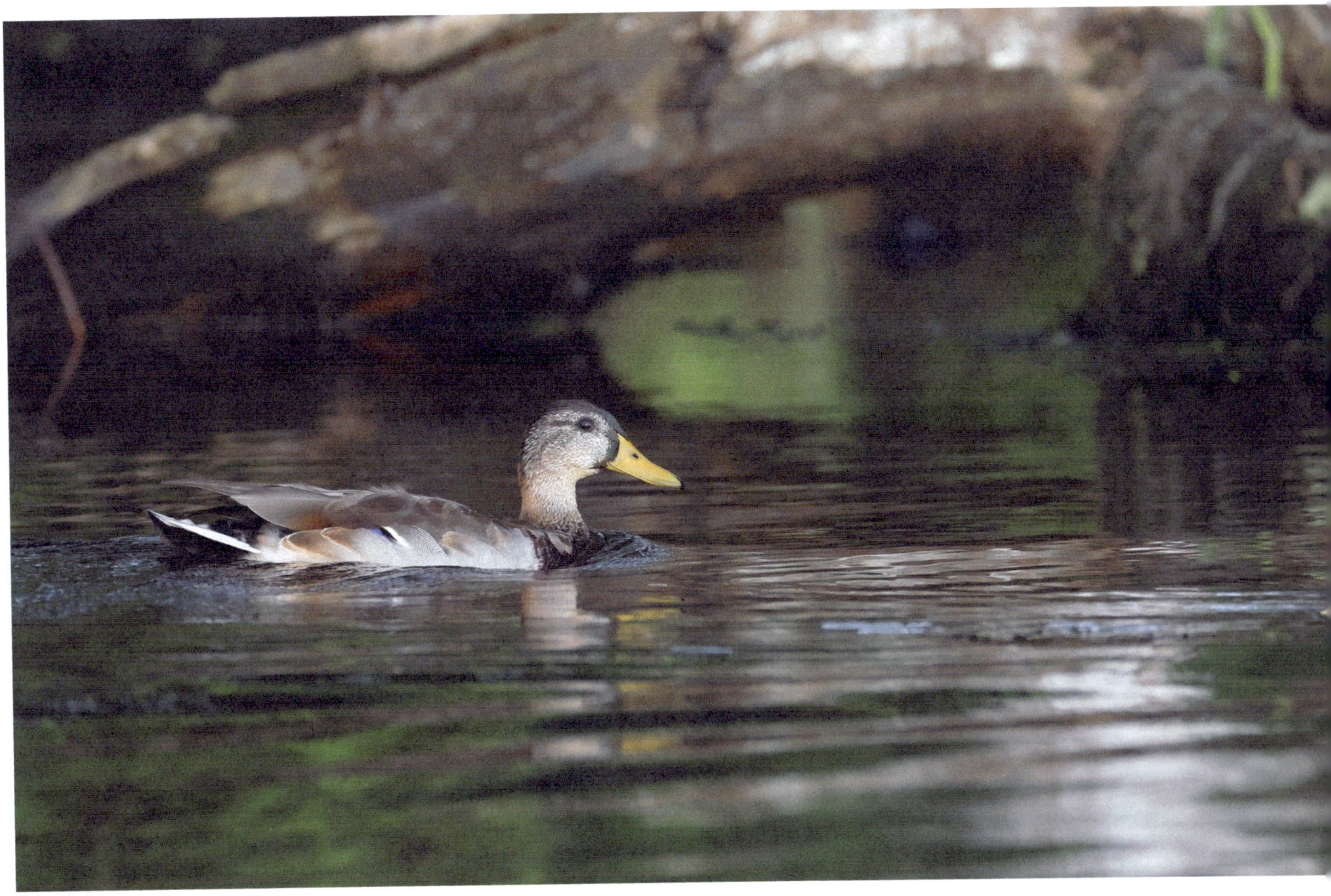

Ducks' prime habitat is areas of water like **ponds, lakes, marshes, rivers, streams, and even oceans**.

But wetlands do much more than provide food and habitat for a plants and animals. They also act as buffers to flooding and erosion, filter contaminants from our water, and serve as key ecosystems in the global water cycle.

Wetlands are also powerful carbon sinks. Wetland plants absorb carbon dioxide as they grow, and when they die, that carbon doesn't get released back into the atmosphere. Instead, plants sink to the bottom of the wetland where they don't fully decompose. That is how carbon accumulates as dead plant matter at the bottom of wetlands. Marshes, peat bogs, swamps can store carbon for hundreds or even thousands of years.

Carbon is an element like hydrogen or oxygen. Carbon can exist by itself, but it can also form molecules, such as carbon dioxide CO_2. Wetland plants absorb carbon dioxide from the air as they grow and use it to build new leaves, stems, and roots. When plants die on land, they decompose and release carbon dioxide back into the air, but when plants die on wetlands, they can't fully decompose and this stops carbon from being released. Decomposition is very slow underwater because there's not a lot of oxygen available. So, as dead plants accumulate at the bottom of the wetland, they retain carbon within them.

Since the industrial age, carbon dioxide levels have been increasing rapidly, causing record high temperatures, but wetlands can help. When we keep our wetlands safe, they absorb carbon dioxide from the air and store it for hundreds of years, plus they provide food and shelter for countless plants and animals.

Do ducks ever get cold?

Watching ducks and other birds walk barefoot on ice and snow, you may feel sorry for them. But ducks have developed very specific body anatomy to deal with cold winter lakes and their chilly watery lifestyle. They do not feel the cold in winter like we do. That's because they have an extra layer of fat. Also, their bodies can restrict blood flow to their feet. As the temperature drops, less blood will flow to ducks' extremities. This is how a duck can swim in frigid water and stand on ice.

Why does a duck stand on one foot?

Have you ever seen a duck standing on just one leg? It's a wonder she doesn't tip over. Ducks often stand on one leg control their body temperature during cold weather by keeping more heat close to the body, the same way people put hands in their pockets when it's cold.

Other birds can do that too. Herons, geese, hawks, and gulls—often maintain a one-legged stance while keeping the other leg tucked up into their body feathers for warmth. And for extra warmth, they tuck their bill into their feathers. This helps them do two things. First, it warms the bird's bill. And, second, by placing their bill under their feathers, ducks can breathe in warmer air.

Do ducks sleep standing up?

Ducks can sleep standing on one or two legs, sitting, or drifting on water. When seated, many species tuck their bill into their feathers, bending their head backward. Like many other birds, ducks are perfectly content sleeping on just one leg. How is that for a comfortable sleeping position?

African black duck

Meller's duck

White-headed duck

The Maccoa duck

Are ducks endangered?

The eight species listed as endangered, meaning they have an elevated risk of extinction, are the **blue duck, Meller's duck, Hawaiian duck, white-headed duck, white-winged duck, scaley-sided merganser, Campbell teal, and Madagascar teal**.

White headed duck

Scaley-sided merganser

Ducks grooming habits

Ducks groom themselves by what we call **preening**. You can often see them plucking their feathers, and cleaning themselves like we would do with combing our hair. Ducks preen to remove all the dust, dirt, parasites. Technically, they take baths every time they go swimming, but they need to keep their feathers waterproof. So, on the back where their tail is, there's a little spot in their tail where there's their oil gland. That is what they're doing. They're touching the oil gland to spread the oil through their feathers and they're sliding it everywhere.

Ducks sleep with one eye open

Ducks and other birds sometimes sleep with one eye open. While sleeping with one eye open, one hemisphere of the bird's brain is awake while the other is sleeping. The awake half allows ducks to watch out for predators.

North pintail

Question: If ducks can sleep with one eye open, are these north pintails awake or asleep?

Ducks have fantastic vision

Like humans, ducks have color vision, and can see red, green, and blue light. But ducks and geese can see a much broader spectrum of colors—from near-ultraviolet to red—than people do. Because their eyes are on the sides of their head, ducks have **panoramic vision**. They can see almost everything around them at once.

Just like people, ducks can't see well at night. But at dawn and dusk, when the world appears dark and fuzzy to us, ducks can see just fine. That's because ducks' eyes are able to process ultraviolet light much better than humans' eyes can.

With eyes set on the sides of their head, most waterfowl look at the world with **monocular vision (each eye is used separately) rather than binocular vision (both eyes view the same object at once)**.

Bucephala-albeola

Ducks are always vigilant

You can never surprise a duck; they are always watching. When sleeping in a group, ducks will almost always sleep in a line. The ducks at each end of the line will keep one eye open to watch for danger.

Quack! Quack! Say what?

The familiar "quack" associated with all ducks is usually the female mallard's quacking, though female dabbling ducks make similar quacking noises. But ducks communicate with more than just quacks. While ducks do not sing, like some other birds, they can make a variety of sounds, including barks.

What most people don't know about ducks is that lots of ducks don't quack. As it turns out, the traditional duck's quack is only made by the female duck.

The drakes don't produce that loud quack, but rather use a softer rasping or wheezing sound. It is more like whisper, compared to the female ducks' loud vocalization.

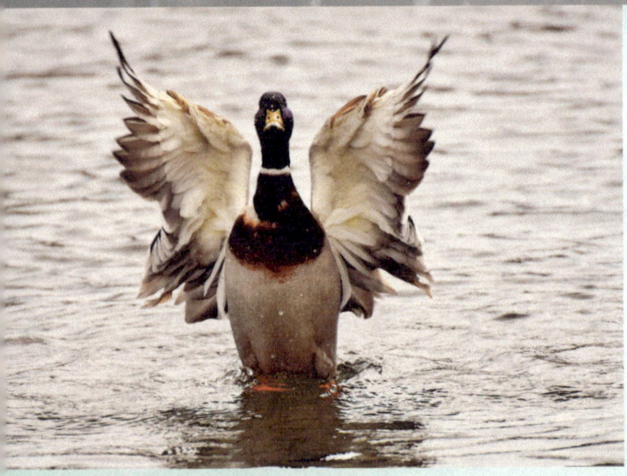
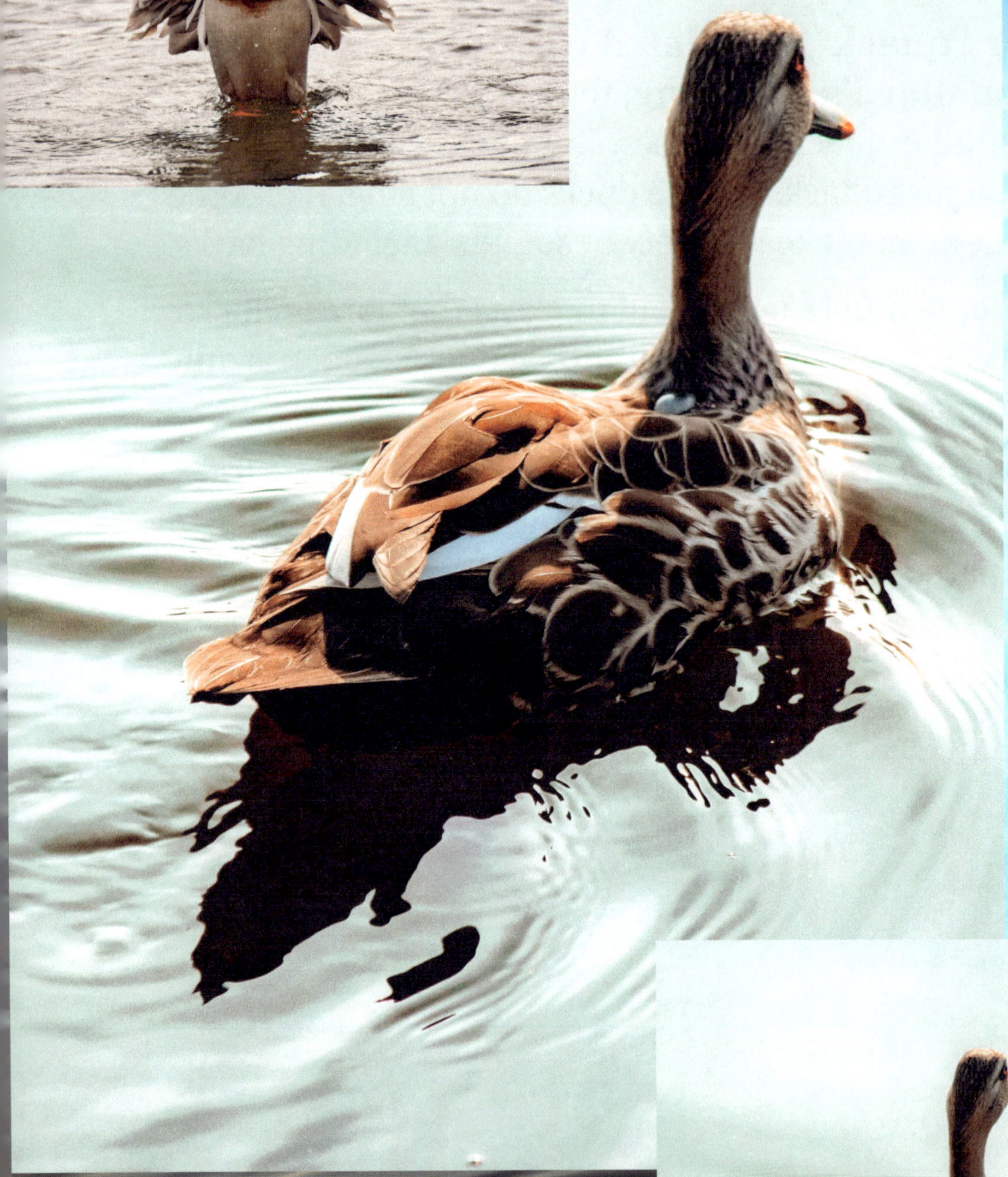

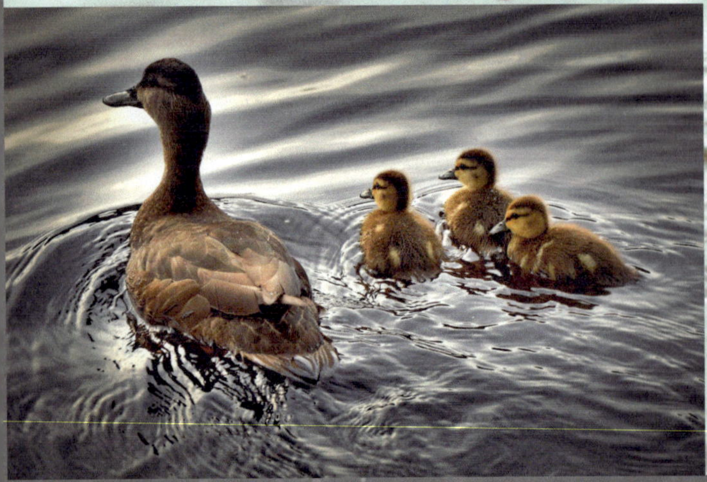
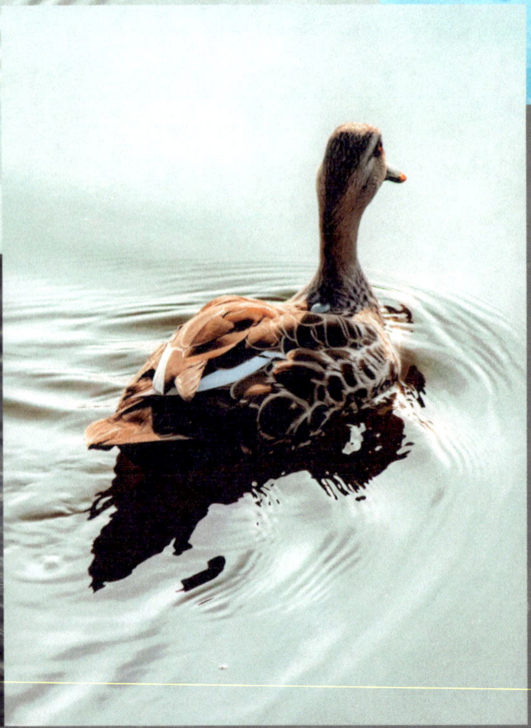

Ducks communicate in complex ways, with each sound having a specific meaning, like their own language.
By making distinct sounds for different reasons, they can pass a wide variety of messages to other ducks, including warnings of danger, mating calls, stress signals, food discovery, or simply letting others know how they are feeling.

Ducks can fly!

You may think—duh, of course, they can, they are birds! But that is not so obvious, since there are many birds who are flightless, meaning they can't fly. Examples include penguins and ostriches, kiwi and the dodo. Kiwi are flightless birds endemic to New Zealand. The dodo is an extinct flightless bird that was endemic to the island of Mauritius, which is east of Madagascar in the Indian Ocean. Chickens and turkeys also can't fly very far, if at all. But ducks are great at flying, and can cover great distances when migrating from one part of the world to another and back.

How do birds fly?

Flight is birds' most important adaptation. It allows them to reach an environment that is inaccessible to most other animals: the air. Birds make flying look so easy; they just take off and fly away. But flying is one of the most complex forms of movement in the animal kingdom. Every aspect of flying—taking off, hovering, and landing—is incredibly complicated. Over millions of years of evolution, different bird species have adapted to their unique environments, developing their wings and flight in unique ways.

> There are various theories on how bird flight evolved, including flight from falling or gliding (downward tree hypothesis), running and jumping (upward ground hypothesis), or wing-assisted running on an incline.

Birds fly by flapping their wings and steering with their tails. Their feathers are light and the shape of their wings is perfect for lifting their bodies off the ground. Besides wings and feathers, birds have other physical characteristics that work together to enable them to fly. They have lightweight, hollow bones, which reduces the body weight. They don't have heavy teeth or jawbones, and have beaks instead. Their large chest muscles allow them to move their wings. Plus, birds lay eggs because they couldn't fly with the weight of their babies inside of them.

Birds have well-developed brains and keen eyesight, so they can react quickly to what is happening. When approaching a tree or cliff, a bird has only a few seconds to choose a spot for landing and avoid crashing. Birds' eyes are much larger in relation to their body size than humans' eyes, and most birds have much better eyesight than humans.

Aren't birds afraid of heights?

It is natural that doing something for the first time can be challenging and even frightening. Although we can't know for sure, it may be that young birds are afraid of making their first flight.

Bird migration: Where do the wild ducks and geese go in winter?

Ducks and geese migrate long distances in search of warmer weather and resources they need to survive and reproduce. Snow buries food or makes it less available, and ice cover significantly reduces habitat available to ducks. Keep in mind that not all winter seasons look the same. The ducks that leave the cold and frozen areas fly up to 800 miles looking for a warm place. The ducks that stay find shelter and continue to look for lakes and ponds that are not frozen.

How do ducks and geese find their way? Ducks and geese follow long pathways from their breeding grounds to wintering areas, on an epic journey that has amazed people for millennia. We are not sure exactly how ducks and geese navigate and don't get lost along the way, but researchers believe the birds use cues from the position of the sun, moon, and stars in the sky; as well as geographic landmarks, such as rivers and mountains; and magnetic fields invisible to the human eye.

Do ducks return to the same place every year? Every fall, millions of waterfowl fly south to warmer weather in search of food and habitat. Some ducks return to the exact location where they nested the previous spring, while others return to the same wintering area year after year. The ability of migratory birds to find these specific locations after being away for several months is known as homing. **Homing** is the ability of an animal to navigate towards an original location through unfamiliar areas. This location may be a home territory, or a breeding spot.
Ducks usually fly at an altitude of 200 to 4,000 feet but can reach even greater heights. A jet plane over Nevada struck a duck at an altitude of 21,000 feet—the highest documented flight by North American waterfowl. Migration is a behavior that requires a lot of energy, which is why ducks often fly at night. Nighttime migration helps them avoid daytime air currents that usually make for rougher flights. Smoother flights mean less energy spent during migration.

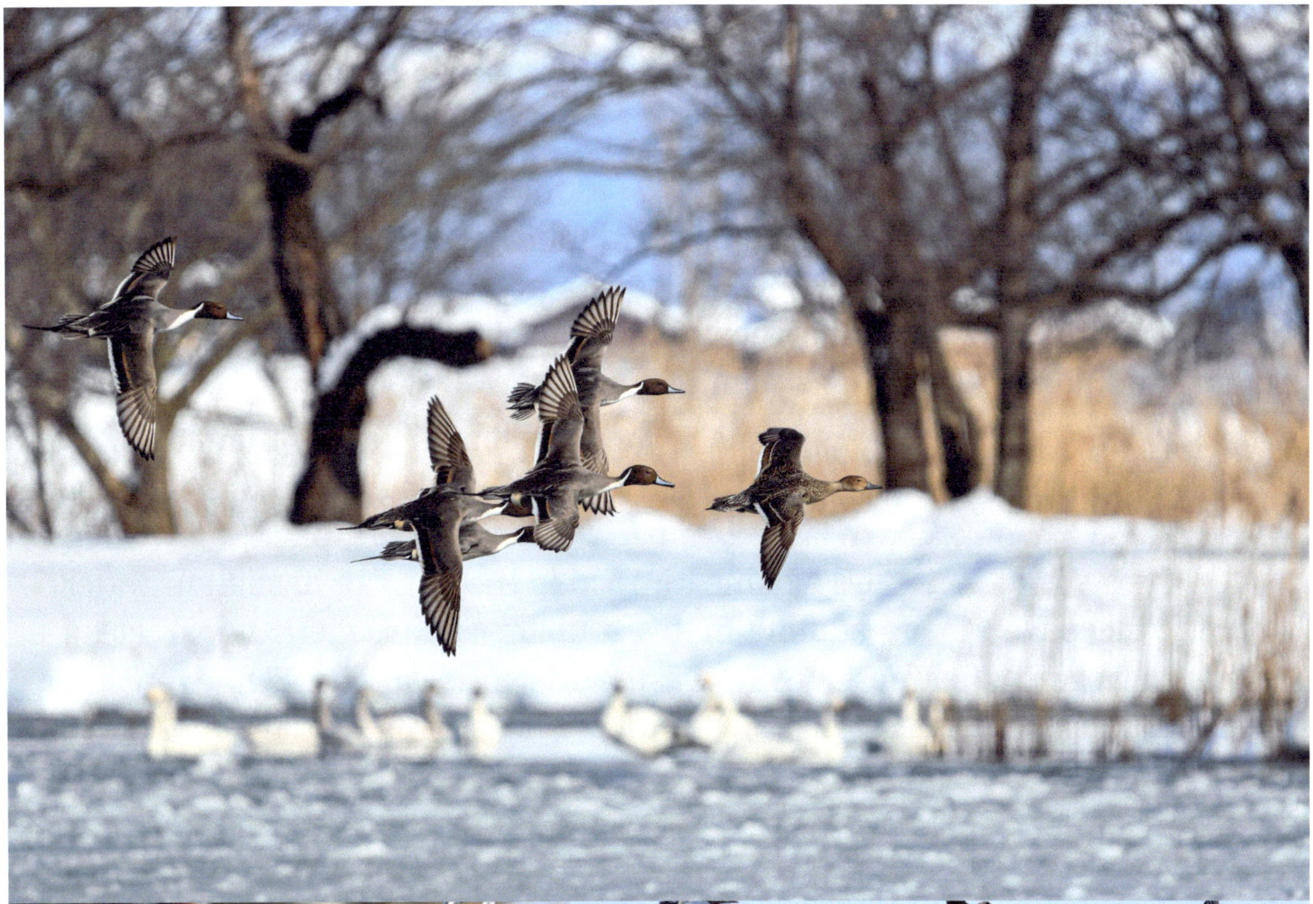

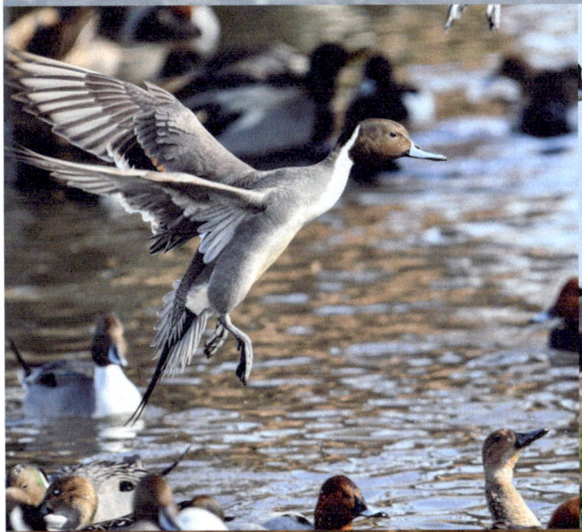

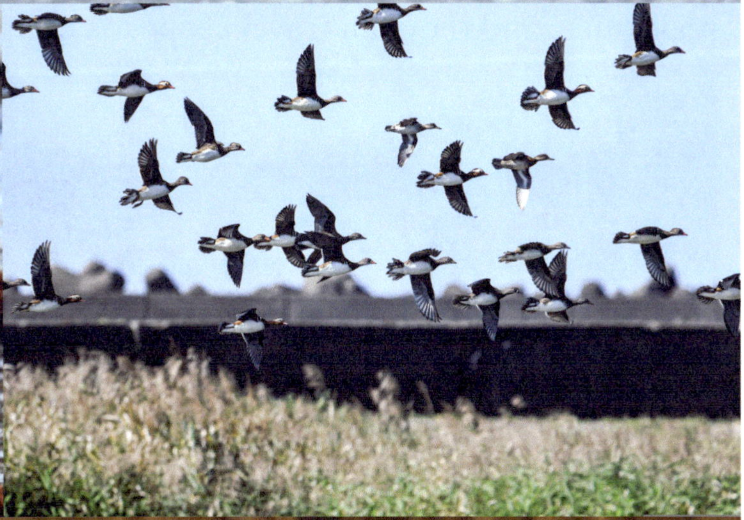

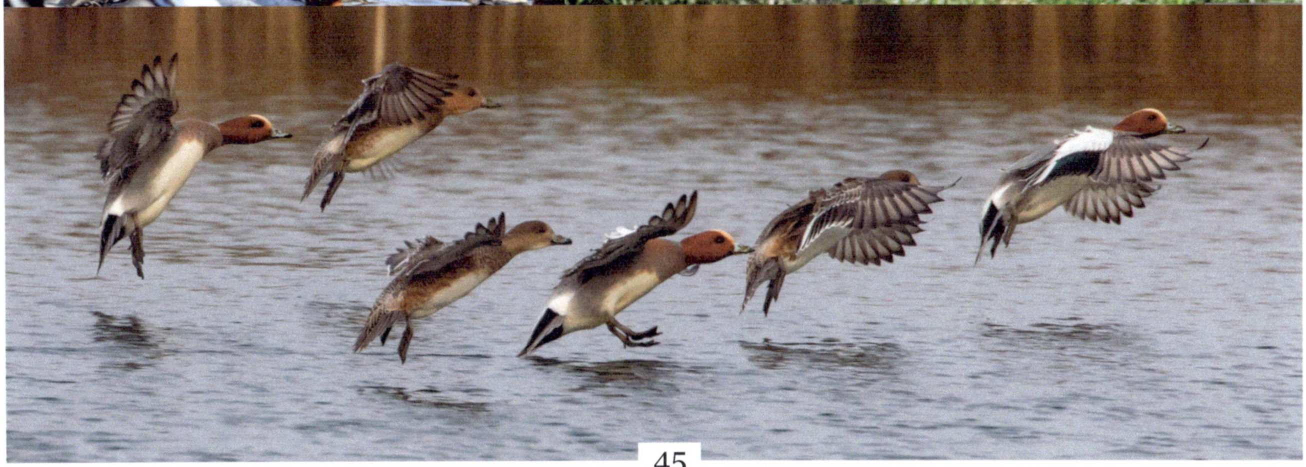

Ducks are social!

Like all animals, ducks love their families and value their own lives. Their social nature means that they're always looking out for their families and for other ducks in their group. In their natural surroundings, ducks spend hours exploring and searching for food. Those not living on factory farms love swimming, flying and walking around, stretching their wings, sleeping and snuggling together, mating and taking care of their young.

Ducks are inquisitive, curious animals who are as intelligent as mammals, such as cats, dogs, and even some primates. They are outgoing, social animals who feel most at ease when they're in large groups, which are called "paddlings" when on water. They spend their days looking for food in the grass or in shallow water, and they sleep with their paddling-mates at night. They're meticulously clean animals who keep their nests free of waste and debris, and they enjoy preening their feathers and flaunting their beautiful plumage for potential mates. In nature, they live for up to 10 years.

Skilled swimmers and fliers, they can travel hundreds of miles each year during their migrations. Like geese, they fly in formation for protection and to reduce air resistance, and they can travel at speeds of up to 60 miles per hour!

Ducks are smart!

Studies have shown that birds are self-aware and can distinguish themselves from others. They learn from one another, such as a duckling learning from her mother which foods are good to eat and where to find them. Ducks can also show complex problem-solving skills. They are very intelligent animals.

Comparing ducks to humans, or even to chickens, crows, or parrots, makes little sense. Just as comparing pigs to dogs (or children), cows to horses, dolphins to fish is like comparing, well, apples to oranges. Animals develop incredible specializations depending on the environment they live in, and making comparisons between species is hardly meaningful.

Ducks evolved to live in one environment, pigeons, crows, ducks, eagles, penguins and parrots in another, and fish, elephants, zebras, monkeys and humans still in another. So what do the experts say?

Pigeons can be taught to distinguish between the paintings of Picasso and Monet. Ravens can identify themselves in a mirror. And crows have been spotted to leave walnuts in a crosswalk and let passing traffic crack them. Many bird species are incredibly smart. Yet among intelligent animals, the "bird brain" often doesn't get much respect.

Birds can complete complex mental tasks, learn from watching each other, demonstrate self-control, and worry about the future. Ducks comprehend cause-and-effect relationships and understand that objects still exist even after they're hidden from view.

How are ducks similar to people?

Just like humans, ducks are capable of feeling a whole range of emotions that are similar to what we feel in similar situations: joy, fear, pain, boredom, fondness, curiosity, aversion, stress, worry, and love.

But the most important thing is this.

> **Ducks are subjects of a life. They are aware of their own existence. They have their likes and dislikes, and have a strong desire to live so they will fight with all their force if anyone or anything threatens to kill them.**

Just as humans, they don't want to die. Ducks and people have more in common than we think! So, what's your favorite thing about ducks?

Relationship with Humans

If ducks could only talk in human language... The things they would tell us would not be pretty! Ducks are exploited by humans in a variety of ways. Wild ducks are killed by hunters and chased away from their natural habitat. The domestic duck or domestic mallard is a subspecies that has been domesticated by humans and raised for meat, eggs, and down feathers. A few are also kept for show, as pets, or for their ornamental value.

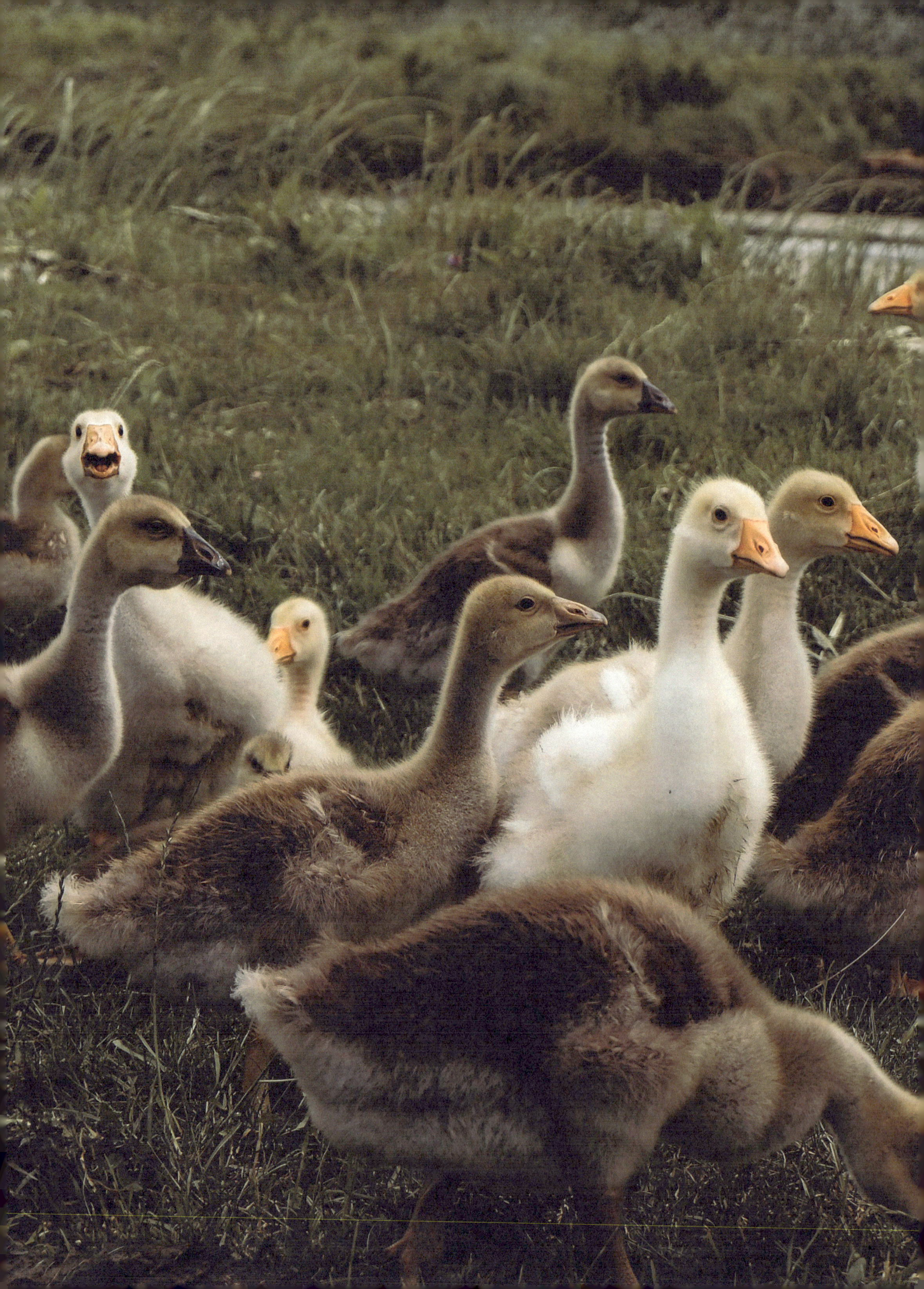

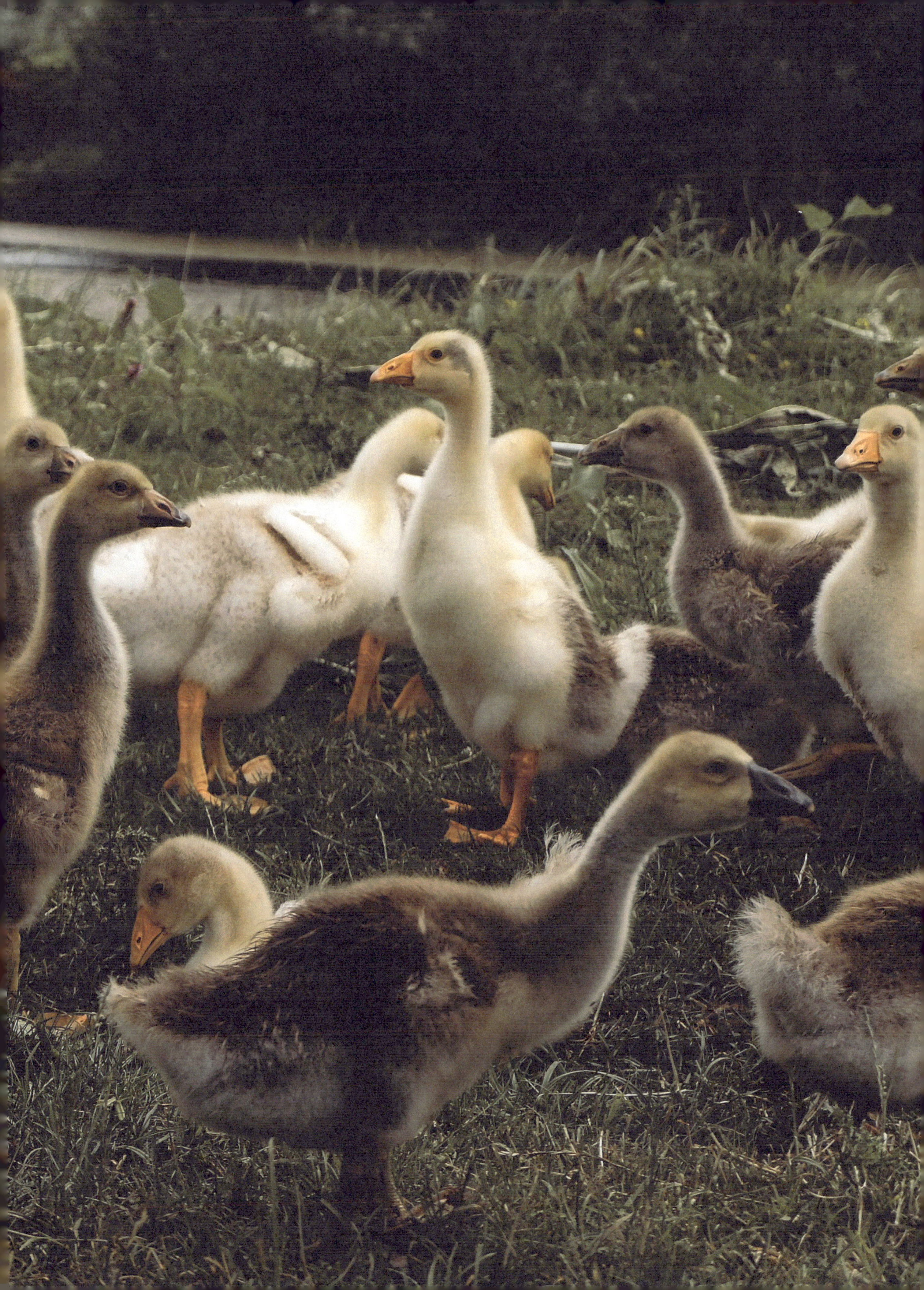

Part 2.
The Hidden Lives of Farmed Animals

Can you believe we raise over 80 billion land animals each year and catch trillions of sea creatures just to eat them? Ducks, chickens, turkeys, cows, pigs, sheep, fish, and other. Yett of us never even see them or get to know them better!

Why? Where are they?

Have you seen a duck today?

You may have seen a wild duck if you live near a river or lake.

But how about a chicken, a turkey, a pig, or a cow?

No?

Me neither!

How is it possible?

Considering that there are so many of them—isn't it kind of strange?

Are they invisible?

Or are they hiding somewhere?

The simple answer is—yes, they are hiding. Or, rather, most of them are hidden from view on commercial farms, and if you wanted to visit them there, you probably couldn't.

It's actually illegal to enter those facilities because the meat and dairy producers don't want us to see what's going on behind those closed doors. You may wonder why, and you'll find out soon enough.
Just keep on reading.

Not Fun Facts about Duck Farms

Being a duck on a farm is no picnic, so don't fall for the cute pictures in books and commercials. Animals in these facilities don't roam freely on green pastures and don't bathe in lakes and rivers.

These amazing and sensitive creatures, whose natural environment is in rivers and ponds where they swim, play, and search for food, are denied these fundamental behaviors when they are stuck in cramped sheds where they live in their own waste.

Millions of ducks and geese are raised on factory farms away from public view to produce fancy "delicacies" for consumers. Foie gras, duck meat, and goose meat bring lots of money to the industry but cause huge suffering for these birds.

Ducks are given some water for drinking, but they can't swim in it or even bathe. Because of the stressful and crowded conditions, disease and filth spread quickly. Many ducks and geese pull out their feathers or peck at one another, so workers cut off the birds' sensitive upper beaks—with no painkillers.

Ducks and geese in the wild never get fat, but these farm birds are bred to be so heavy that they can't even walk right. They can never swim, fly, build nests, or raise their young, as they would normally do in nature. In fact, many ducks and geese raised for food won't ever see the light of the sun or breathe fresh air.

The way they make foie gras is especially traumatic for these birds. They force feed them until their livers grow up to 10 times bigger than normal. ("Foie gras" means "fatty liver" in French.)

Even 'free-range' and 'organic' labels don't mean a better life for farmed animals. For starters, only a small minority of animals live on such farms. Plus, sadly, these animals usually face similar conditions as those on factory-farmed ones.

Fortunately, we can all help end this cruelty, and you'll soon learn how.

.

Ducks are subjects of a life. They are aware of their own existence, have their likes and dislikes, and show a strong desire to live so they will fight with all their force if anyone or anything threatens to kill them or their young.

55

Eat, Drink, and Poop

But that's not all. The meat industry is a major contributor to many environmental problems, such as **pollution, deforestation, loss of biodiversity, and depletion of soil and water**. Raising and killing billions of animals for meat on factory farms each year produces enormous amounts of waste and excrement. Animal agriculture leads to widespread land and water pollution. Because animals are often fed massive amounts of antibiotics and additives, these chemicals are also found in high concentrations in their poop, which means that fecal pollution from animal farms is especially disastrous for the environment.

Another problem is that raising animals for food requires a lot of resources. Two-thirds of all agricultural land in the U.S. is used to raise animals for food or to grow grain to feed them. So, if all the grain currently fed to farmed animals in the United States were consumed directly by people, the number of people who could be fed would be almost 800 million.

The production of 1 pound of high-quality animal protein requires feeding 6 pounds of plant protein to livestock, which creates a huge strain on land and water resources, plus it increases greenhouse gas emissions, associated with animal agriculture.

It may be the "traditional" way of doing things, but is it's definitely not the most efficient and smartest. Why can't we do what's more sensible, especially in light of all the recent concerns about environmental degradation and climate change? Switching to plant proteins in the diet can help to supply adequate high-quality protein for the global population and may reduce the potential for adverse environmental consequences.

So, perhaps it's time for a change...

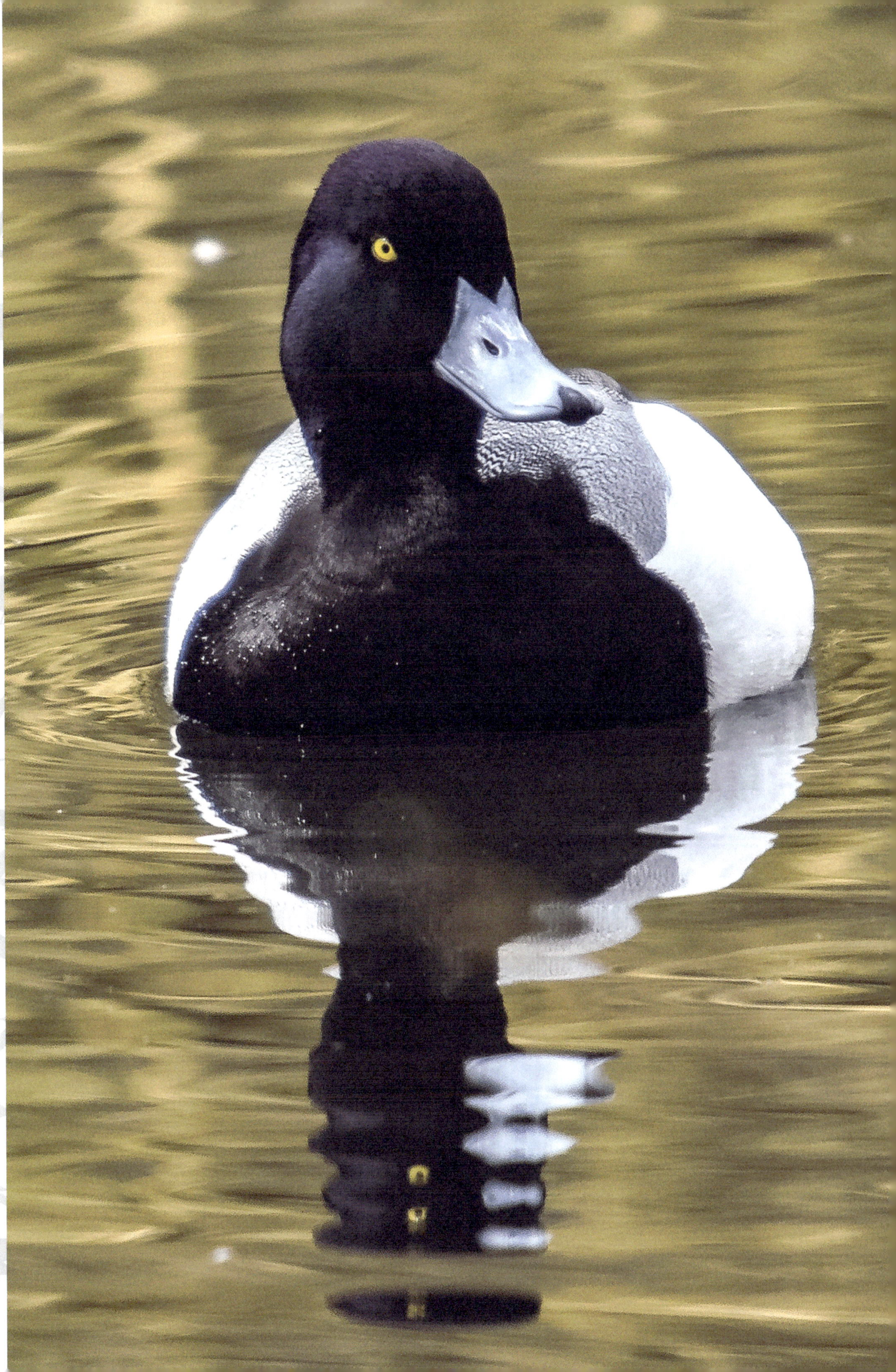

More habitat for wildlife

There are now more than 8 billion people on Earth. Human activity has harmed the environment in many ways, and some of the damage may be irreversible. A big problem is that human activity leads to a loss of biodiversity. Biodiversity is the variety of the animals and plants in any environment.

Plants are killed, and animals either die or have to find a new habitat. Sometimes entire species become extinct. Biodiversity is important because all the plants and animals in an ecosystem each play a role in keeping the ecosystem alive and healthy. To protect biodiversity and our own future we must provide more habitat for wildlife. So how do we do this? And where can we find so much free land? Three initiatives that address this need are 30 by 30 Goal, Half Earth, and the Plant Based Treaty.

30 by 30 Goal

Over 190 countries have reached an agreement to protect and conserve at least 30% of world's land and ocean by 2030. This took place in December of 2022 at the United Nations' COP15 biodiversity summit in Montreal, Canada. Almost a third of the world's land and oceans, including forests, peat bogs, coral reefs, and other precious areas, are set to be protected by the end of the decade under this landmark global treaty for nature in order to "halt and reverse biodiversity loss" by 2030. The agreement aims to slash subsidies that are harmful to nature—for example, those supporting unsustainable agriculture or fisheries, and provide more protection for indigenous people.

Half-Earth

Half-Earth is an ambitious project, calling to protect half the land and sea to provide sufficient habitat to reverse the species extinction and ensure the long-term health of our planet. Who came up with this idea? Edward O. Wilson (1929–2021), who was recognized as one of the leading scientists in the world. Why half? When 90% of habitat is removed, the number of species that can persist sustainably will diminish by half. If 10% of the remaining natural habitat is removed, most or all of the surviving species would likely disappear, many of them forever. If, however, half of the global surface is put under protection, 85% or more of the species will survive. How do we know which half to protect? The key thing is to protect the right areas. Fortunately, the latest technology allows us to map the exact geospatial location and distribution of the species of our planet so that we know where we have the best opportunity to protect the most species.

The Plant Based Treaty

The Plant-Based Treaty is a grassroots campaign calling on world leaders to take action on one of the biggest drivers of the climate and biodiversity crisis: our food system. Eliminating fossil fuels is a must, but it will not be enough to stop climate change, and it won't fix the other sustainability issues, such as loss of biodiversity, degradation of soil, pollution of water, deforestation, and depletion of our oceans.

Three 'R' principles

The Plant-Based Treaty is asking governments around the world to take radical steps to shift away from animal agriculture to slash emissions and protect biodiversity. The campaign wants world leaders to create a new treaty to transform the food system, centered on three "R" principles, which are: **Relinquish** - to stop expansion of the animal agriculture industry; **Redirect** - to shift away from animal-based foods, such as meat and dairy, towards plant-based diets; and **Restore** - to restore and protect the key ecosystems for Earth's biodiversity.

The IPCC's (the Intergovernmental Panel on Climate Change, a body of the United Nations) latest report and other scientific findings make it clear that rapid reductions in greenhouse gases are needed now. We cannot wait two, five or ten years. We must transition to a plant-based food system immediately if we are to reduce methane to safe levels and slow global warming. Animal-based foods represent the most carbon-intensive and resource-hefty products driving the majority of the food system's emissions, mostly due to methane. Globally, livestock farming makes up almost 20% of the world's greenhouse gas emissions and 70% of arable land use. What we can do is bring back the forests that we cut on the land that we are currently using for grazing animals and growing food for livestock. This way we may be able to stop and even reverse climate change.

EAT PLANTS PLANT TREES
Endorse the plantbasedtreaty.org

Learn more about Plant Based treaty and ask your family members and local politicians to endorse it! Young people just like you are taking action all around the world, so you won't be alone.

The Human Herbivore Diet

All our favorite foods can be made from plants. All it takes is shopping in a different isle of your grocery store and ordering plant-based items from the restaurant menu. Is that too much to ask?

What is the best diet for humans?

Although many of us choose to eat both plants and animals, which is the omnivore diet, **humans are anatomically herbivorous**. Vegetables, fruits, nuts, seeds, grains, mushrooms and legumes are the basis of a healthy plant-based lifestyle that is kind to animals and the planet.

And the truth is—**what we eat is entirely our choice**.

Even people who eat lots of meat and consider themselves carnivores—are not obligate carnivores. A carnivore is an animal that thrives on a meat-based diet, while an **obligate carnivore** requires a meat-based diet in order to survive. While carnivores may eat other sources of nutrients, such as plants and fungi, obligate carnivores are unable to get the nutrients they need from plants.

Humans have the characteristics of herbivores. Unlike lions or tigers, we are not genetically destined to eat meat, which means we can get all the nutrients we need from plants. We have short, soft fingernails, not claws, and our canine teeth are small and blunt and have no chance of tearing animals apart. We aren't suited to eating raw meat or cooked meat, as it is linked to a wide range of health problems, including heart disease, diabetes, and cancer. The Academy of Nutrition and Dietetics confirms that a well balanced vegan diet is healthy for everyone. Books by many doctors and dietitians, provide resources for kids and adults on how to be healthy by eating plant foods. Today, most humans are still omnivores, but the **number of human herbivores, a.k.a. vegans, is snowballing.**

If you are not an herbivore yet, how about becoming one today?

Do humans need duck protein to live?

Our bodies need protein to live. Protein is an essential part of the diet, but do we need duck protein to survive? Now, that you've learned so much about ducks, you may wonder if ducks need to be killed for humans to thrive. So let's find out. But first, let's answer the question—

What is a protein?

Protein is an essential nutrient required for the building, maintenance, and repair of tissues in the body. All proteins are composed of **amino acids**. The amino acids are the chief building blocks of proteins; that means, proteins are made by putting various amino acids together into specific combinations.

There are dozens of naturally occurring amino acids, but all proteins in our body are derived from just twenty. Of these twenty amino acids, our body is able to make only twelve. They are called **nonessential amino acids**. Nonessential means that our bodies can produce it, even if we do not get it from the food we eat. The other eight amino acids must be obtain from food. These eight amino acids that we must get in our diet are called **essential amino acids**. Our body can recycle the essential amino acids, but it cannot produce them. This means we must have to provide them to body through diet. Our bodies need these raw materials in the form of essential amino acids to replace the everyday losses.

What are the best sources of proteins for humans?

Plant protein is the healthiest source of protein for humans. Scientists found that replacing red meat with plant protein reduces risk of premature death because of chronic disease. A diet of sufficient caloric intake based on fruits, vegetables, nuts, whole grains and legumes will provide an optimum intake of protein and other nutrients, 30-70 grams per day, depending upon the foods eaten.

A variety of grains, legumes, and vegetables can provide all of the essential amino acids our bodies require.

Healthy plant protein sources (in grams):

Black beans, boiled (1 cup) 15.2
Broccoli (1 cup) 3.7
Bulgur, cooked (1 cup) 5.5
Chickpeas, boiled (1 cup) 14.5
Lentils, boiled (1 cup) 17.9
Peanut butter (2 tablespoons) 7.2
Quinoa, cooked (1 cup) 11.0
Seitan* (3 ounces) 18
Spinach, boiled (1 cup) 5.4
Tempeh (1/2 cup) 16.8
Tofu, firm (1/2 cup) 12.5
Whole-wheat bread (1 slice) 4.5

But eating the protein-rich foods is only the beginning. Our body can't use the big proteins molecules in food until they're broken down into amino acids and peptides by our digestive system. These amino acids and peptides become the raw materials from which our body can build all the proteins that it needs.

Is there ever a risk of protein deficiency?

As long as the diet contains a variety of grains, legumes, and vegetables, protein needs are easily met, without any meat, dairy, or eggs, and there's no risk of protein deficiency. In fact, protein deficiency is almost unheard of in the United States.

So, do humans need duck protein to live?

No, we don't! Since protein is widely available in all plant foods, we don't need to eat ducks or any other animals at all.

How to become an herbivore

It's easy! When it comes to becoming an herbivore, everyone can do it at their own pace. The important thing is that every time you choose plants, you are taking a step in the positive direction. Here are some tips on how to get started:

It's easy! Here are some tips on how to get started:

1. Identify the plant-based foods you love

You may be surprised to discover how many of the foods you already enjoy are plant-based, including stir-fry dishes, soups, pastas, sandwiches, grain-based breakfasts such as granola and oatmeal, not to mention the huge variety of plant-based dishes from international cuisines such as Indian, Chinese, Japanese, Thai, Mexican, Middle Eastern, Italian, and African.

2. Find replacements for foods you eat often

If you like cereal for breakfast, try it with different plant-based milks, such as oat, soy, almond, rice, hemp, or other. If you like burgers, choose a plant-based burger made from beans, veggies, or mushrooms. If you like pancakes or waffles for breakfast, choose a recipe that is dairy- and egg-free (using mashed banana or applesauce instead of eggs). If you enjoy chili for lunch, use your usual recipe, but only with beans or swap animal ingredients for plant-based substitute.

The point is—whatever food you enjoy, you can find a plant-based version that has the same look, convenience, and even taste. Focus on options that feel familiar before jumping into unfamiliar ingredients and dishes. This is easy to do when cooking at home. To eat plant-based while dining out, research and ask about ingredients or find restaurants with many plant-based options. Ask when those alternatives aren't available; most chefs will accommodate your requests and may even add those items to the menu.

3. Stock your pantry with plant-based foods so you have plenty of options when hunger or cravings strike

When people think of a plant-based eating, they may picture themselves living on salads and brown rice—which is not a very appealing scenario for most of us. So, besides having a wide variety of fruits, vegetables, beans, mushrooms, grains, nuts, seeds and spices, get some plant-based milks, cheeses, veggie burgers, burritos, pizza, nut butters, and other goodies. The food should taste good and fill you up. It's more important to enjoy your new way of eating than to drudge through bland meals and snacks that leave you unsatisfied.

4. Make it into a game

You'll be surprised at how diverse plant foods can be, with thousands of new flavors, textures, and combinations to try. Rather than dwelling on what's not available, treat it like a fun activity such as a puzzle, research project, or ingredient hunt (like an Easter Egg Hunt, only you do it in a grocery store, farmer's market or online). Imagine yourself as a hero standing up for animals—which you are.

5. Don't be hard on yourself

You may feel like giving up, because *it's never going to work*. It takes time to form new habits and judging yourself will not help. Also, feeling isolated may make you question your choices. You may ask yourself: *Am I the only one that loves animals and tries to do the right thing?* Remember that you're not. The number of herbivores is growing fast, and you are not alone.

Remember why you're doing this—for the animals, other people, and the planet. Read books, watch movies, get to know some amazing animals, and make friends with people who practice this kind of lifestyle every day.

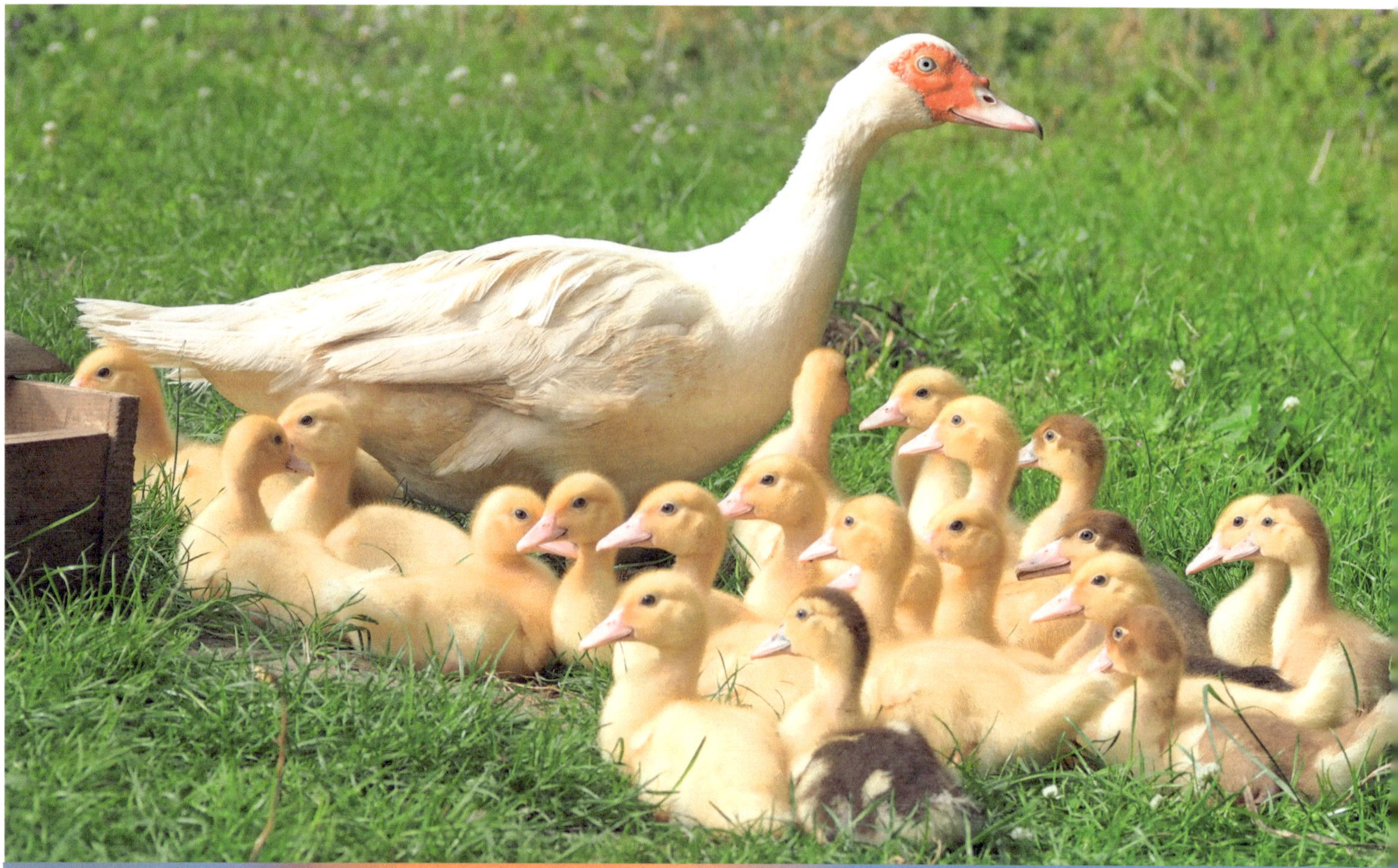

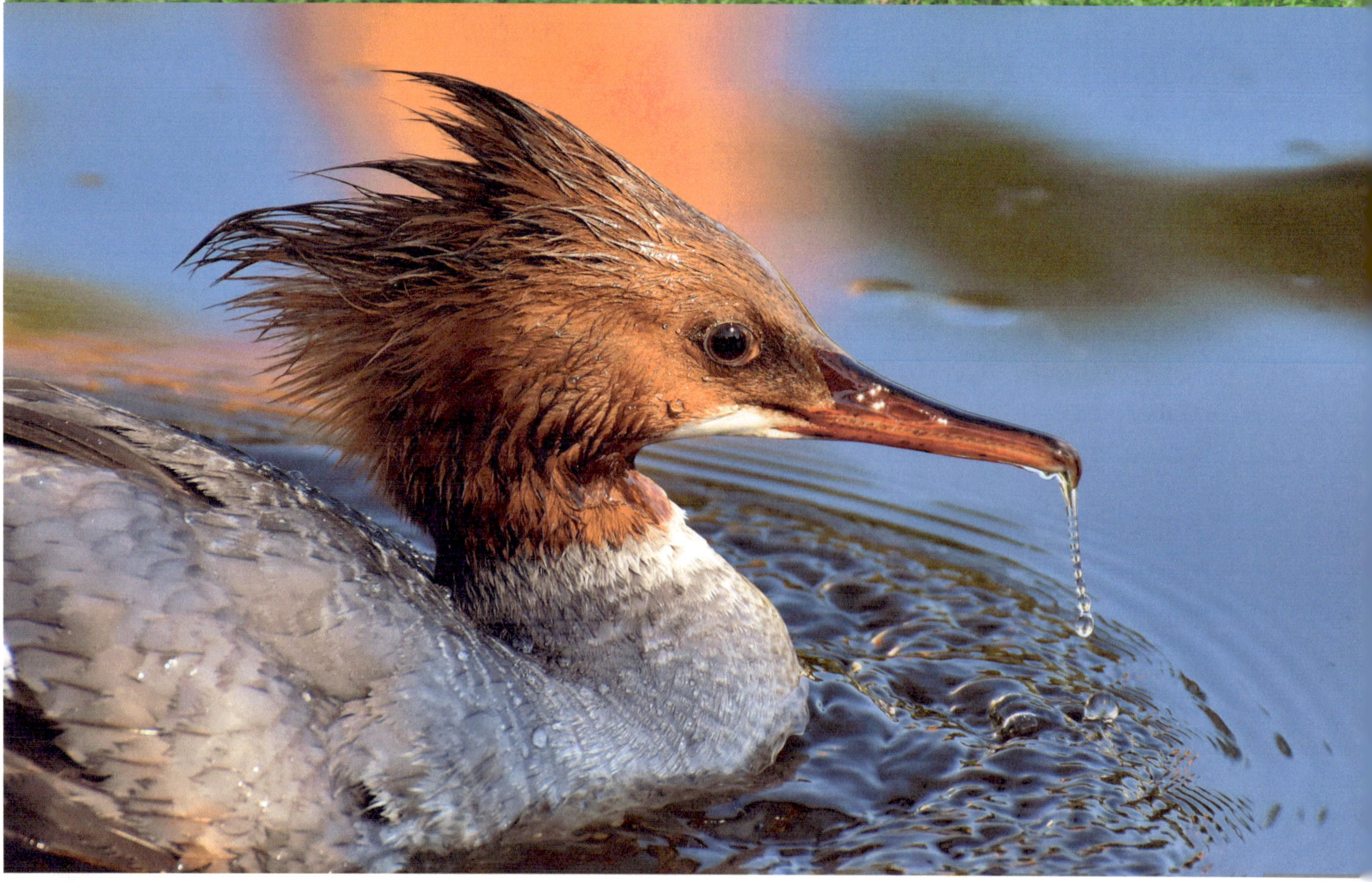

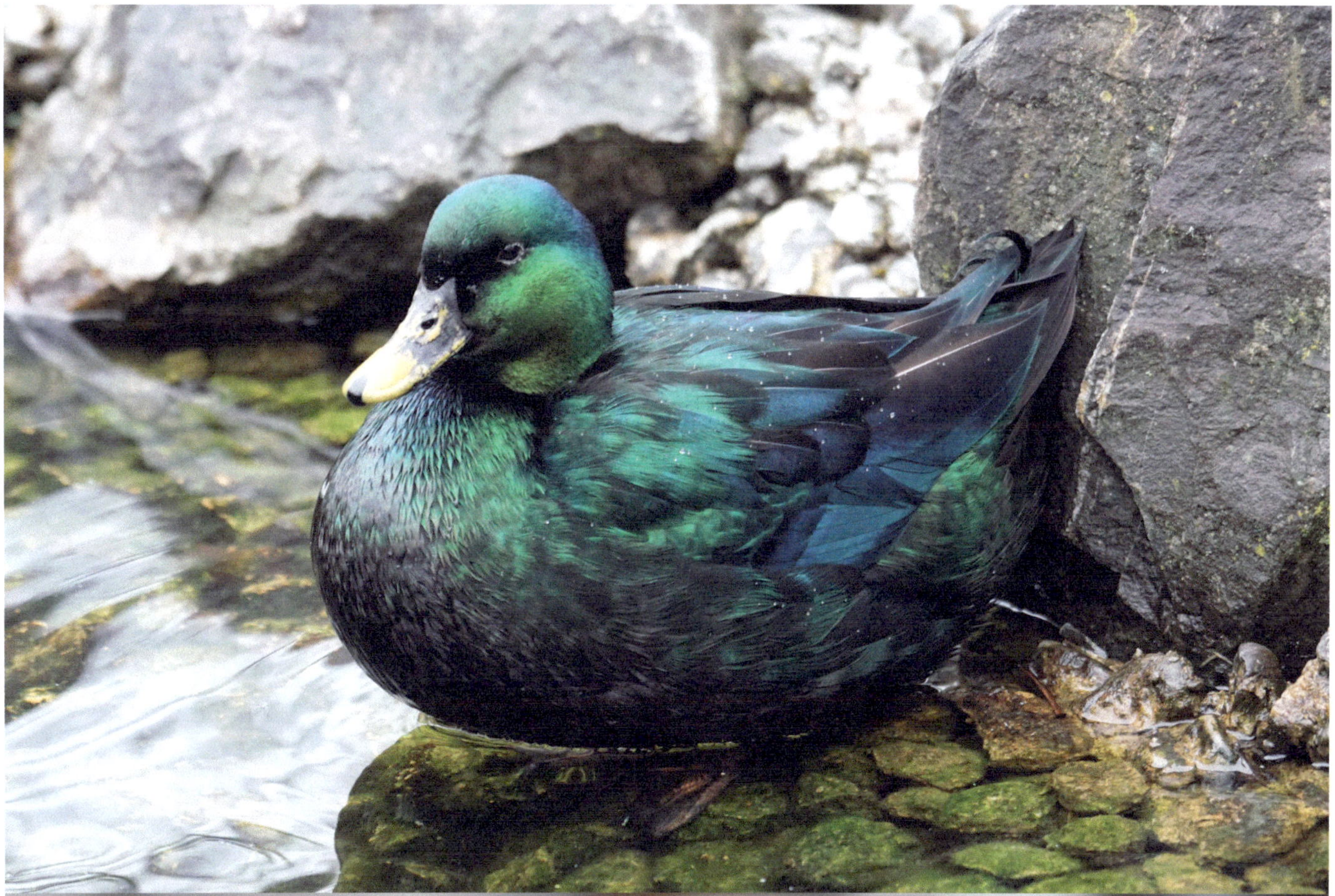

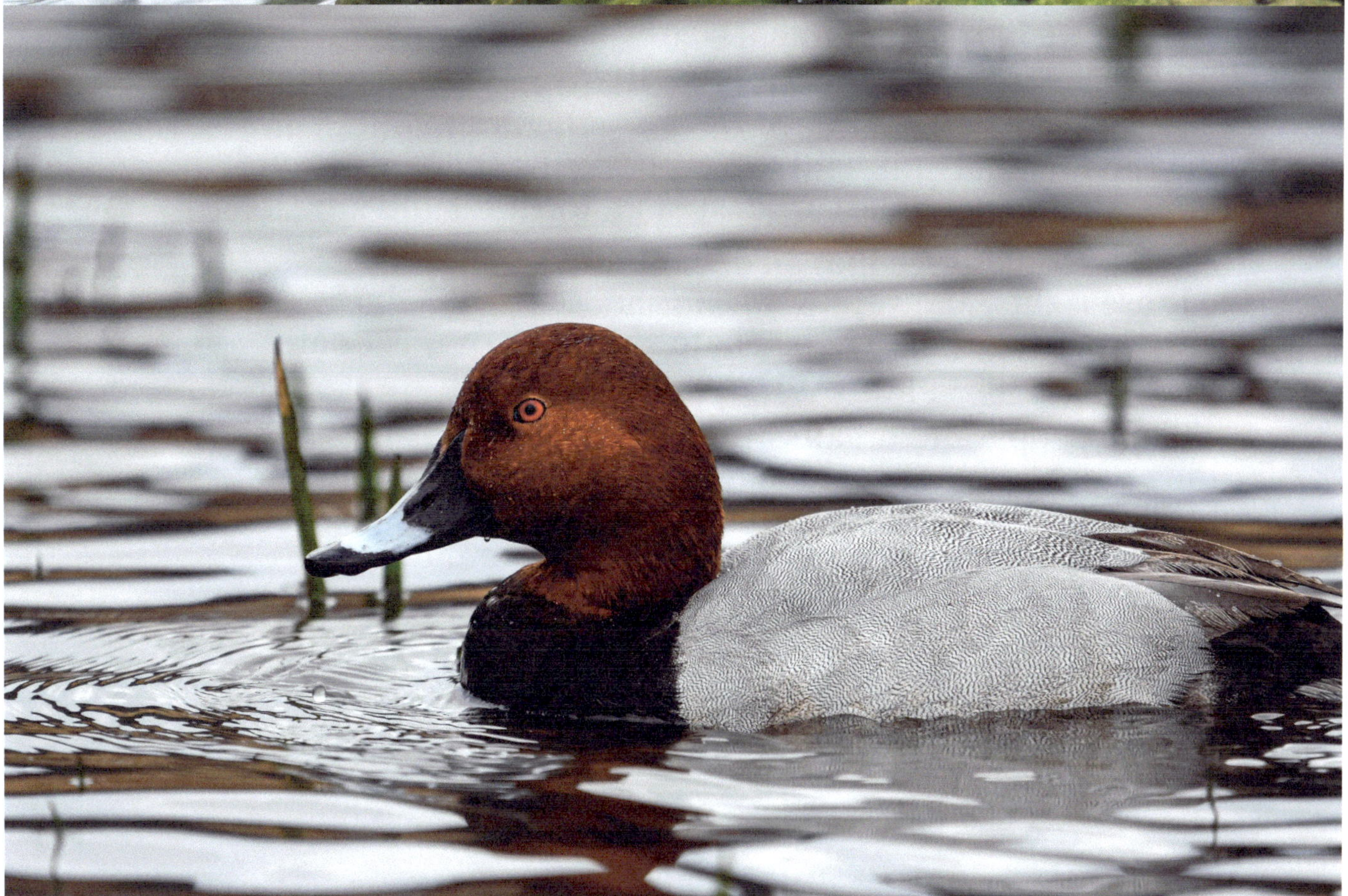

Part 3. Should ducks have rights?

In the first chapter, we've shown you that, in many respects, ducks are similar to people. So much so that animal activists talk about giving them certain rights.

But what do they mean, exactly?

Rights—to what?

Should ducks have the same rights as humans?

That sounds silly, doesn't it?

Well, not really.

When we talk about animal rights, we're not talking about ducks having the right to vote, drive a car, or go to college.

We're talking about ducks and geese (and other animals) having the fundamental right to live, not to be treated as things or property, and not to be caged, shot at, tortured and killed.

Most people agree that all ducks—and all animals—should have those rights, and yet—when we choose to eat a duck, a goose, a chicken, a pork chop, a ham sandwich or meatloaf— our actions are the opposite of what we believe.

Some people and organizations are striving to make animal farming more 'humane,' selling meat that is "free-range," "natural," etc. But making the cages a little bigger, or providing ducks with a bit more space reduces suffering, but doesn't address the heart of the problem.

After all, what does the word *humane* mean to you?

"To examine whether something is 'humane' first determine whether you would want it done to you," said Andrea Kladar.

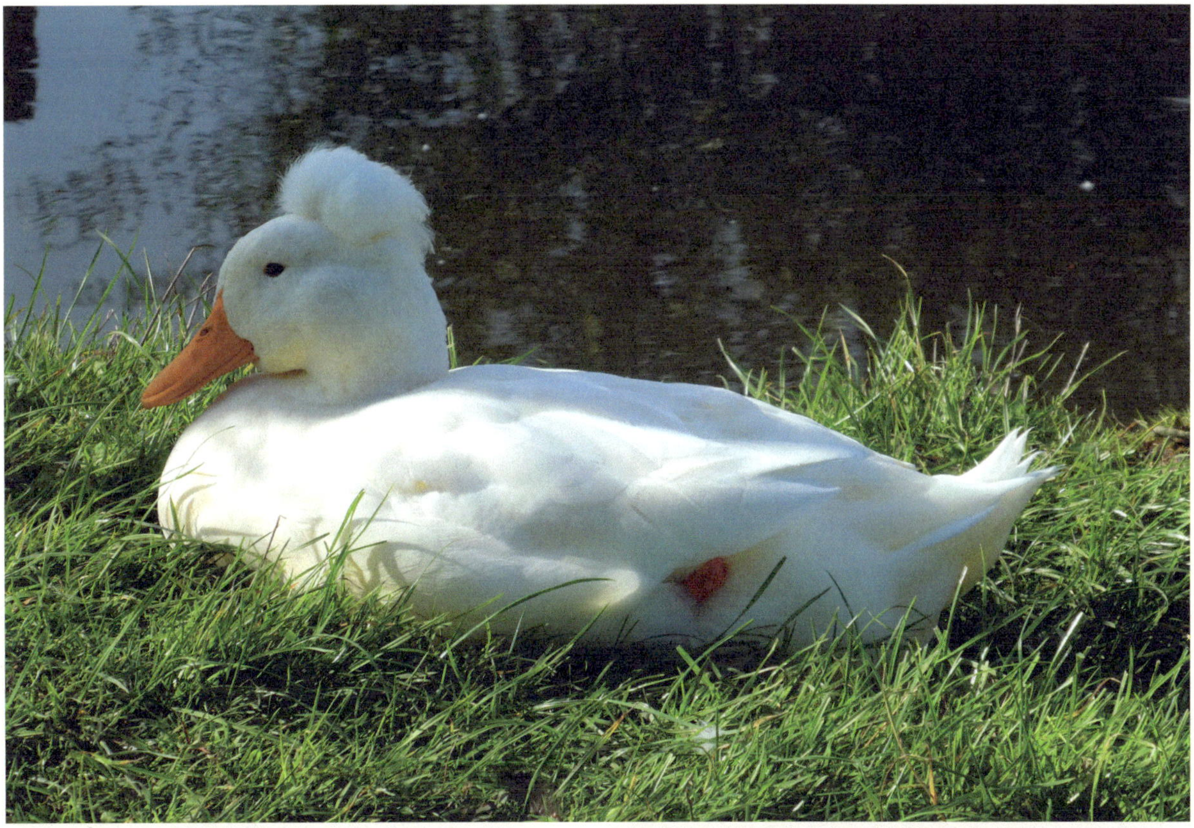

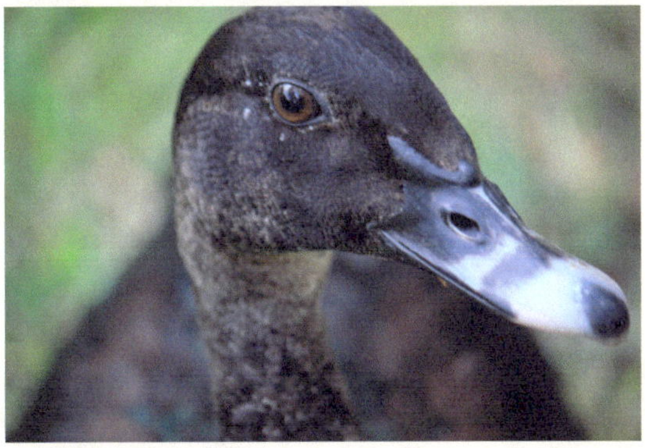

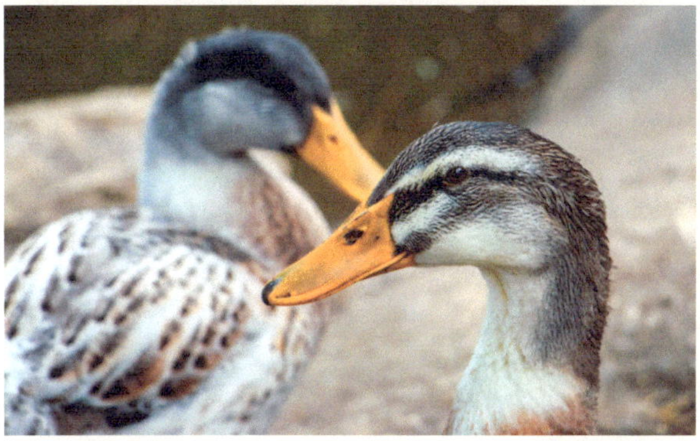

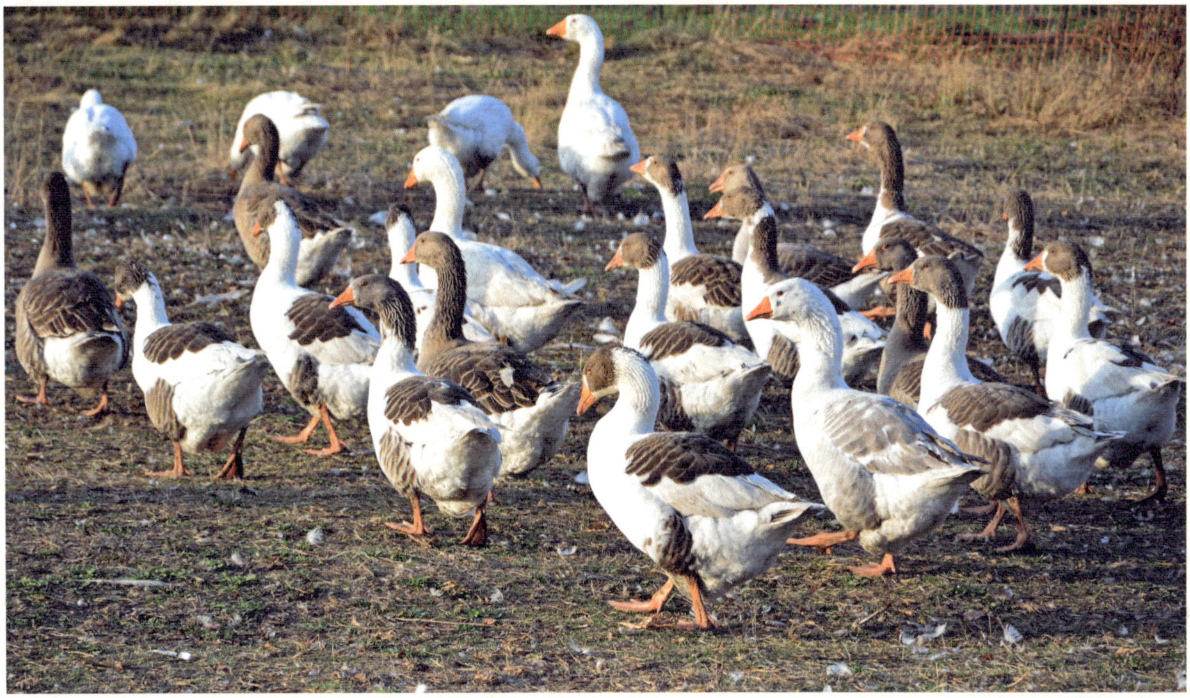

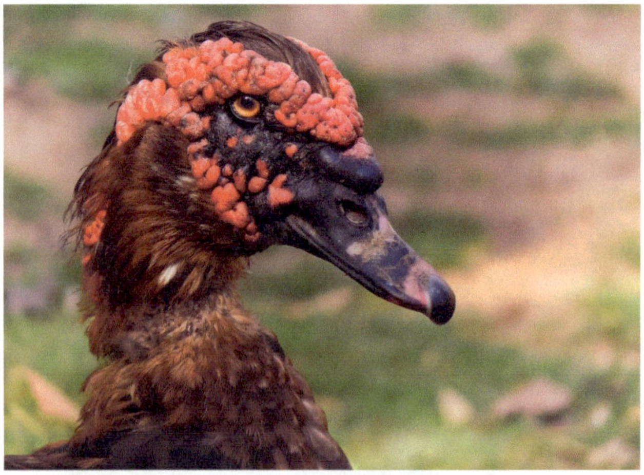
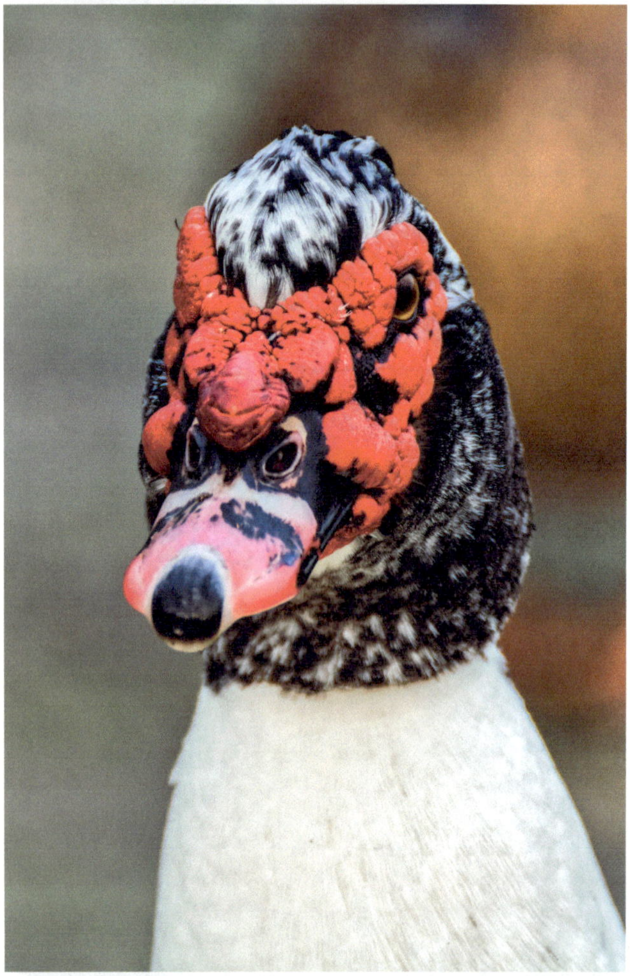
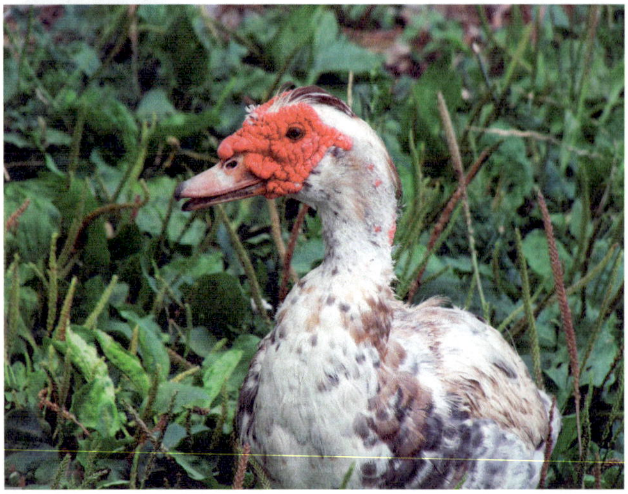
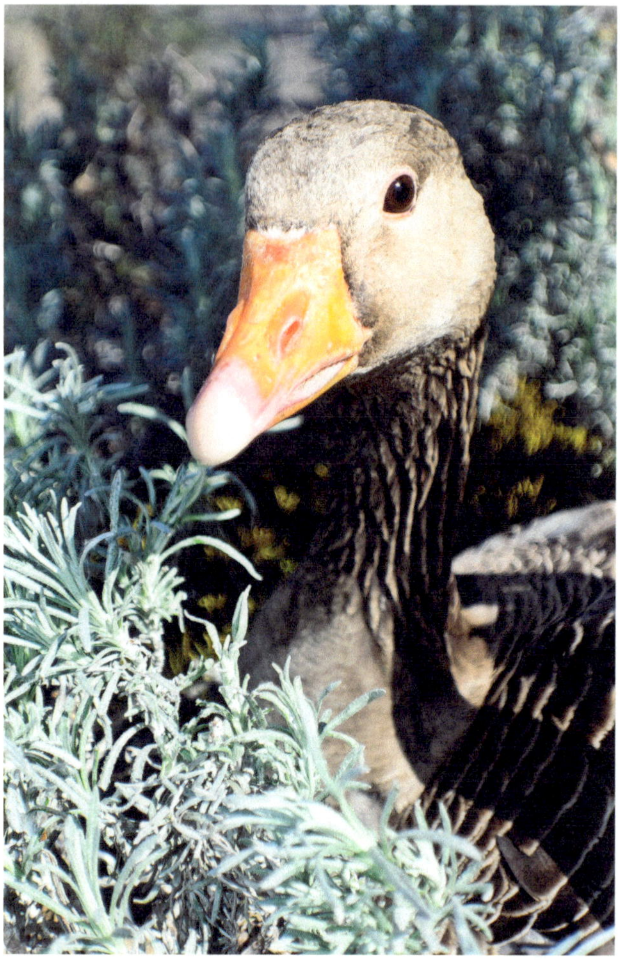
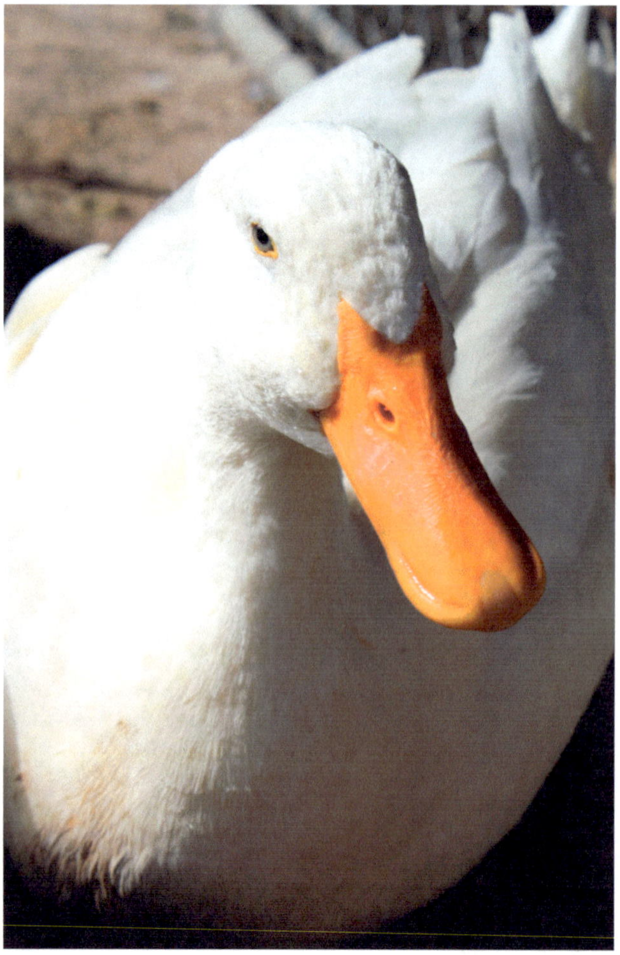

Someone, not something

"Only prejudice allows us to deny others the rights that we expect to have for ourselves. Whether it's based on race, gender, sexual orientation, or species, prejudice is wrong. If you wouldn't eat a cat, why eat a duck or a cow? Cats, dogs, ducks, cows or chickens have the same capacity to suffer, but it is prejudice based on species that allows us to think of one animal as a companion and the other as dinner."

Animals don't have voice and can't defend themselves. They will not put up a fight to demand that their basic rights, such as the right to live free from bodily harm and not be killed, be written into official laws and enforced.

That is why we must do what animals are unable to do.
And that's what animal rights activists are trying to do.

"I live to see the day when animals have the right to run if they have legs, have the right to swim if they have fins, have the right to fly if they have wings." Gretchen Wyler.

Animal rights are not just some ideology or philosophy. It is a social justice movement that challenges society's traditional view that animals exist solely for human use. Supporters of animal rights believe that animals have an inherent worth, a value beyond their usefulness to humans. And that every creature with a will to live has a right to live free from pain and suffering.

Duck sayings: how many do you know?

The word duck comes from the Old English noun meaning "diver" or "dive", because of how ducks find food by going bottom up.

like water off a duck's back

Ever heard the phrase "like water off a duck's back"? It usually means a criticism has no effect on the person being criticized. After all, water really just rolls off a duck's back, thanks to their waterproof feathers.

preening

Preen /priːn/: preening, (of a bird) tidy and clean its feathers with its beak. Of a person, devote effort to making oneself look attractive and then admire one's appearance. Similar: pretty oneself, groom oneself, tidy oneself, spruce oneself up, doll oneself up, or plume oneself.

'bird brain' is a compliment!

You may have heard this saying describing someone who's silly, but bird brains are far more humanlike than once thought. As you havelearned, birds are smart, so if when calling someone a "bird brain," make sure you're using it as a complement.

If it looks like a duck, walks like a duck and (etc.) like a duck, it probably is a duck

The **duck test** is a form of reasoning, when a person can recognize an unknown subject by observing that subject's characteristics.

take to something like a duck to water

If you take to something like a duck to water, **you discover you are naturally good at it or that you find it very easy to do**.

getting ducks in a row

To get your ducks in a row means to organize your tasks and schedule so that you are ready for the next step. There are several theories behind the origin of this expression. Real ducklings, of course, walk in a line behind their parent, and the expression ducks in a row certainly brings that image to mind.

to duck out

To duck out means to leave suddenly and usually telling no one.
They ducked out on us without even saying goodbye."

duck and cover

To duck and cover means to hide under something and cover your face and head as a way of trying to protect yourself.

Can we use the words "someone" and "anyone" for animals or just for humans?

Calling an animal a "thing" or "it" is the default in English. But if you have a special animal in your life that you think of as a member of your family then you likely call refer to your pet as "he" or "she". In that case, you could use the human-like term "someone". So which approach should you choose?

Despite what some people will tell you, you can say whatever you want. And when you do, it reveals something about your attitude. Do you think of animals as more like people or more like things? If you think of animals as being like humans and describe them like humans, then of course you would use the words "someone," "he," "she," or "they" (if the gender is unknown), regardless of whether the animals is your pet or not.

More duck-related words

duckling, bird, water, mallard, paddle, swim, waddle, water bird, waterfowl, fowl, broadbill, feather, beak, avian, wing, flight, fledged, fledgling, webbed, migrate, aves, clutch, float, aquatic, coot, plumage, sheldrake, drake, egg, quack, quacking, ruddy duck, Muscovy duck, merganser, pintail, goldeneye, canvasback, shoveler, bufflehead, gadwall, bummalo, redhead, douse, teal, musk duck, scaup, eider, rubber duck.

But what will happen if we stop eating animals?

If we stop eating animals, they will either overrun the earth or—worse yet—go extinct! Both scenarios sound pretty bad, but if we think about it, they really aren't. First of all, it's unlikely that all people will stop eating animals at the same time, so as the numbers of vegans and vegetarians increase, the numbers of farmed animals will decrease. It's the law of supply and demand. Fewer people buying meat, means farmers raising fewer animals, and switching to growing plants, restoring wetlands, forests, and biodiversity or finding other ways to make money.

But if everyone stops eating domestic animals—they may even go extinct! We worry all the time about species going extinct, but would that be bad? Not at all! Even if domestic animals go extinct, wild animals will still be here, as long as we provide them with a sufficient natural habitat to thrive.

Ducks Need You!

Ducks need YOU!
Animals need YOU!
Ducks need your help!
Animals need your help!
Don't say you can't do anything.
You are more powerful than you think.
You show your power—with a knife and a fork.
Every day, three times per day—or more.
You have the power to stop eating animals.
Think you couldn't live without animal flesh and eggs? You can!
Animals on the other hand can NOT.
We take everything from them—their flesh, their eggs, their feathers.
And of course their lives.
Time to be a Hero for animals is NOW!
Because if not you—then who?
If not now—then when?

77

Crossword Puzzle

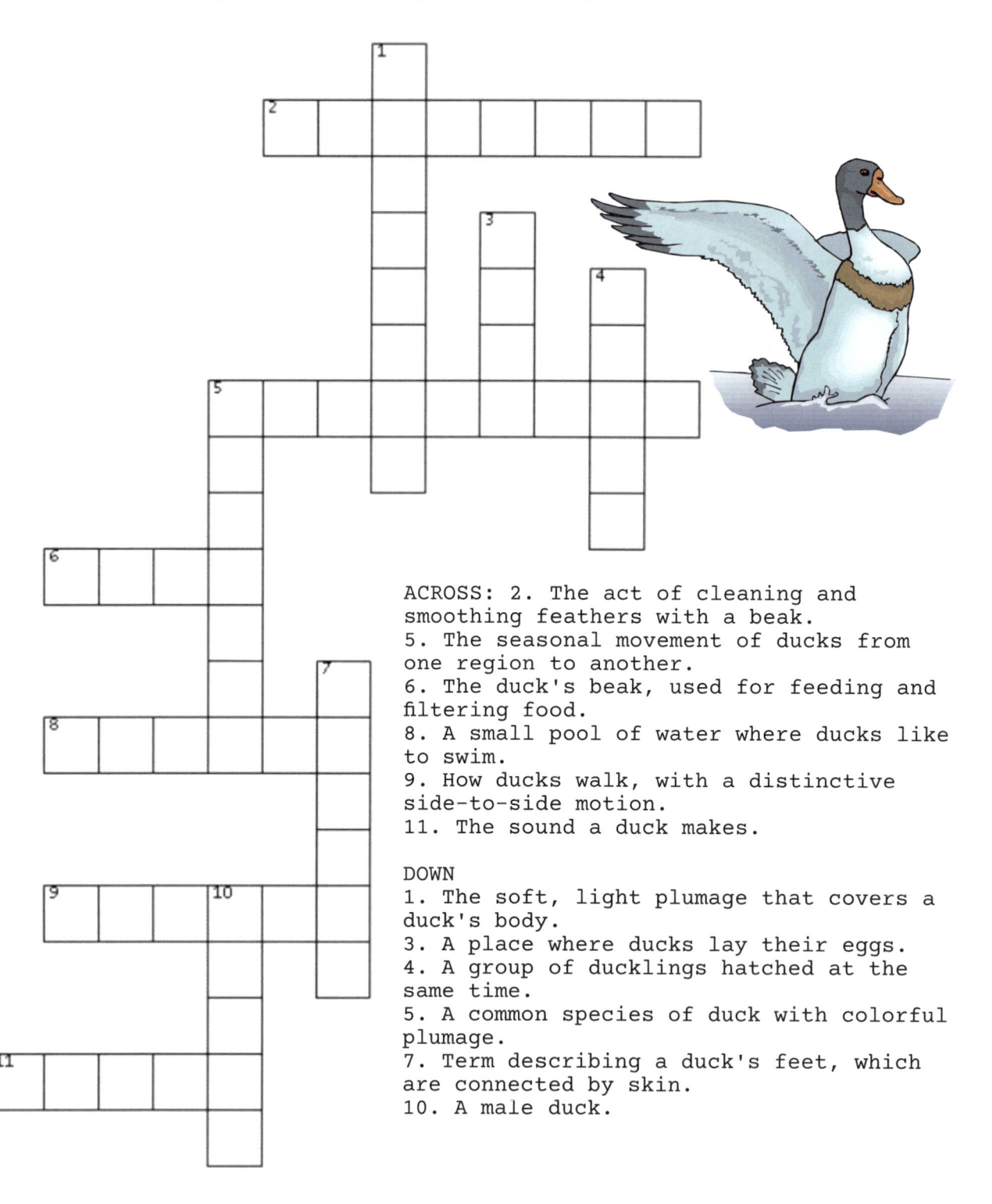

ACROSS:
2. The act of cleaning and smoothing feathers with a beak.
5. The seasonal movement of ducks from one region to another.
6. The duck's beak, used for feeding and filtering food.
8. A small pool of water where ducks like to swim.
9. How ducks walk, with a distinctive side-to-side motion.
11. The sound a duck makes.

DOWN
1. The soft, light plumage that covers a duck's body.
3. A place where ducks lay their eggs.
4. A group of ducklings hatched at the same time.
5. A common species of duck with colorful plumage.
7. Term describing a duck's feet, which are connected by skin.
10. A male duck.

Quiz Time!

Reading fun facts is addictive! Hope you had as much fun reading them as we had compiling them! And even the not-so-fun facts are good to know—because knowledge is power. We have the power to change the things that we don't like—to make this world a better place for all.

1. **What is the primary purpose of a duck's bill (beak)?**
   A) To help them hear sounds underwater
   B) To regulate body temperature
   C) To aid in flight
   D) To forage for food

2. **Why do ducks migrate during certain seasons?** A) To escape predators B) To find mates C) To search for better nesting sites
   D) To find food and suitable breeding grounds

3. **Which of the following is NOT a common species of duck?**
   A) Mallard
   B) Peking
   C) Wood Duck
   D) Barn Owl

4. **What is the term for a group of ducks flying together in formation?** A) Flock
   B) Gaggle
   C) Herd
   D) School

5. **Do ducks have teeth?**
   A) Yes, they have sharp teeth for catching fish.
   B) No, they do not have teeth.
   C) Yes, they have flat molars for grinding food.
   D) Only their beaks are toothed.

6. **Why do ducks often turn upside down in the water when feeding?**
   A) To cool off on hot days
   B) To practice acrobatics
   C) To reach aquatic plants and small invertebrates beneath the water's surface D) To avoid predators

7. **What is the purpose of the oily coating on a duck's feathers?**
   A) To make them waterproof
   B) To deter predators
   C) To help them fly faster
   D) To keep them warm in cold water

8. **What is a common behavior of mother ducks with their ducklings?** A) Abandoning them shortly after hatching B) Teaching them to fly immediately C) Leading them to water and providing protection D) Leaving them to fend for themselves

9. **What do ducks typically eat in the wild?**
   A) Berries and fruits
   B) Insects, small fish, and aquatic plants
   C) Leaves and tree bark
   D) Only aquatic algae

10. **Do people need duck protein ?**
    A) Yes, it's a crucial part of a balanced diet B) No, people can get protein from other sources C) Only if they want to quack like a duck

Word Search

```
W O L E J S D G B I R D W J S
M A G A E P N C B V E I A Z X
Y G T L P I K R N U G Y T H E
J V C E L T O Z A S F M E F E
Z I O K R A F L I G H T R G A
A R C C D F I D V D N P F M D
B U W B S U O K A Q F L O K L
D L I P I U G W A Q C U W H D
K L P H D N M S L E U M L S M
L M S I I K C A U Q B A J V Q
B H S W R E H T A E F G T Z Y
B Z Z T L F R K K W Q E L I I
D V V Q C C B C V B F F W D C
Z H Z P W B G T Y C G E Y T O
A B X A Y G D Q W K I I Y Y N
```

duckling   feather   aquatic
bird   beak   plumage
waterfowl   avian   egg
waterfowl   wing   quack
broadbill   flight   Muscovy

Read More Books

Thank you for reading! If you enjoyed it, please leave us a glowing review. To find more books, ebooks, audiobooks, quizzes and activities, go to : JoannaSlodownik/kids

```
Answers: Quiz: D) D) D) A) B) C) A) C) B) B)
Crossword: 1. Feathers 2. Preening 3. Nest 4. Brood
5. Migration, Mallard 6. Bill 7. Webbed 8. Puddle 9.
Waddle 10. Drake 11.Quack
```

Made in the USA
Thornton, CO
11/25/23 20:50:20

23fcc4fb-a19c-4c6b-95f3-16e5a0208b46R01